THE SOULOLO(

GRIT

STORIES OF EMPOWERMENT, INSPIRATION, COURAGE, AND STRENGTH

THE SOULOLOGY CHRONICLES

GRIT

STORIES OF EMPOWERMENT, INSPIRATION, COURAGE, AND STRENGTH

NATASHA AZADI | DR. CRAIG BEACH | LISA CARTER | KIM MURPHY
MARTIN REID | CARL RICHARDS | LISA RIZZO | STEPHANIE ROBINSON
ROE SARITA | KRISTINA SHEA | CAITO STEWART | MARIYA TARASIO

SHP

Star House
PUBLISHING

For any information regarding permission and bulk purchases contact:

www.starhousepublishing.com or email
info@starhousepublishing.com

ISBN PAPERBACK   978-1-989535-54-7
ISBN HARDCOVER   978-1-989535-55-4
ISBN E-BOOK   978-1-989535-56-1

Printed in the United States of America
First Edition, 2022.

Design by: Susi Clark | Creative Blueprint Design
Edited by: Akosua (Jackie) Brown

CONTENTS

Grit is that 'extra something' that separates the most successful people from the rest. It's the passion, perseverance, and stamina that we must channel in order to stick with our dreams until they become a reality.

TRAVIS BRADBERRY

NATASHA AZADI

Natasha Azadi is a multi-published author with her first book being: The Soulology Chronicles: Voices. She a grieving mother, a private maternity nurse, and soul coach. After the passing of her daughter in 2016, Natasha set out to help others globally with their losses and grief. She is a passionate, intuitive and spiritual healer with multiple certifications as a Soul Coach, Reiki Practitioner and in Meditation. She was born and currently lives in England and travels for work throughout the United Kingdom.

AGAINST ALL ODDS

NATASHA AZADI

There are two ways of spreading light:
To be the candle or the mirror that reflects it.

EDITH WHARTON

What is mental illness? It's a common question. Many struggle with their mental health and do all they can to hide any illness from friends, family, work colleagues because of the stigma attached to it. Why? What is there to be ashamed of? Easy for me to ask… yet, I too, have hidden my mental illness, addictions, and diagnoses from many, in fear of being judged. I was afraid it would have a damaging effect on my career.

SECRET SHAME

At the age of twelve, I realized something was wrong with me. I was always teary, sad, and run down. I was a quiet child, so more often than not, I was overlooked. No one paid close attention to me because I was the good kid, the one that never got into trouble or did anything wrong. What was under the radar was that I was also so hungry for the love and attention of my family. I wanted to feel like I belonged somewhere, but nobody could see it. Sadly, I wasn't brave enough to speak out about my needs.

The only thing I wanted to do was go to school and write in my journal. At age twelve I also started self-harming. I was so unhappy with myself, my family and my life. I felt that it was the only way I had power and control over myself. I liked to feel the pain of the blade as it cut through my flesh, because it actually made me feel something and it gave me a release. I kept it hidden for a long time by wearing long tops, and never wearing dresses or skirts. My arms and legs were always covered.

As much as I liked the pain, I felt immense shame, which in turn made my depression worse. I am sure that my family noticed at some point, but nothing was ever said or done. So I carried on in secret.

I moved in with my dad and stepmom and by the time I was fourteen, I was not only still cutting, I was also heavily bulimic, chronically depressed, and always tired. My stepmom somehow guessed what I was doing and confronted me. They intervened and tried to get me help, but it was short lived. In the UK, although the National Health Service provides free health care, its mental health resources are very poor. I was given six weeks of one-hour therapy sessions and at the end of them, was told to take some pills as they would make me better. But they didn't. After that, there was no further support, other than at school where I had a mentor and saw the school nurse regularly.

My parents didn't understand. My dad told me I was selfish and asked why was I doing this to *them*, especially since they had taken me in from my mother and given me a good life. I could not answer him as I didn't quite fully understand why I was hurting myself either. I just knew I hated myself so much, but did not know why.

I felt lost and ashamed. All I wanted was my family to see me and to love me. I never felt I had that. Knowing now how much my parents both struggled emotionally from their own upbringing, I can understand their reaction, but it was also deeply unfair to have their emotional baggage and wounds projected onto me from birth.

Overtime, things calmed down. But again, the calm was short-lived. I stopped cutting myself and finally reached a healthy weight. After an argument with my parents, and being as stubborn as I am, I left home at sixteen and never went back. I stayed on friends sofas until I was able to rent my own place. I was juggling school while working three jobs at one point to keep a roof over my head and food in my belly. Life was stressful.

In order to help cope with my stress, I found alcohol; it became a great comfort, as a blanket of sorts. I was constantly partying, spending the nights out drinking. To keep up with work and college, I started to take diet pills and stimulants to counteract my tiredness. My weight plummeted to a record low. Before I knew it, I was seventeen, in my last six months of college, and a mess. I was extremely unhappy and depressed. I felt alone. I believed that I had nowhere to go, and no one to turn to.

DARK HIT

Life had a way of taking jabs at me, and my coping mechanisms, were not the healthiest. It was in late 2007, when my life took another dark hit. After a night out of partying, I arranged to stay with a friend instead of going home. As usual, the party continued at her house. As everyone was bopping and I was tired and not really into the party, I shut myself into a guest room to go to sleep. I awakened when I felt someone climbed into the bed with me. I was sexually assaulted.

It took me a long time to come to terms with what had happened that night. I was paralyzed with fear during the encounter—I just froze. The main thing I remember are silent tears rolling down my cheeks. I told only a select few about my trauma. I never spoke out and I never sought help.

I shut off emotionally for a long time and was only able to function when I was drunk. I did what I needed to at the time to be able to survive and I don't regret that. I let that night control so much of my life for a very long time.

MY CANDLE BURNED OUT

At twenty-one years of age, after a whirlwind romance, I got married and was happy. After many years of infertility, we were elated to find out that we were finally pregnant. However, after having my daughter Jessica in 2012, my mental health plummeted. Again, I found myself having days feeling on top of the world, while on other days I couldn't stop crying. I blamed hormones, and refused to see a doctor. My way was to handle things by myself.

I believed that I didn't need to involve a *"Dr. Someone"* who I feared might say that I was crazy, or worse, an unfit mother.

I put so much pressure on myself to be the perfect mother, to give my child everything that I never had. It was so important to me that my child would come from a loving and stable home, with two parents, but by 2016 my marriage had fallen apart. A couple of months later, in September of that year, my four-year-old daughter Jessica died after an accident at home in the garden. I loved her with every fiber of my being and of course, I always will. I felt like my candle had burned out.

I was alone, in shock, and in deep grief. My entire world had crumbled. I was a shell of the person that I once was, spending my time lost in my own dark world, in constant pain. My weight was at an all-time low. I didn't care about myself—I just wanted to die. I fantasized about every way I could kill myself. I was constantly drugged up with pills from the doctors, as I had been diagnosed with depression, insomnia, PTSD, and anorexia by then. I hid myself away from the world.

Eventually I came back. Everyone figured I was coping, as it appeared that I was getting on with my life. They had no idea how depressed I was nor how many pills a day I was taking. I learned that my anorexia was my way of having some control: subconsciously, I figured that at least I could control my weight as everything else was overwhelming. I had lost everything and I could not change that, but I had full power over my weight, or so I thought at the time. My family and friends didn't know what to do for me. They could see how much pain I was in, but they couldn't give me back my daughter, the one thing I desperately craved.

I smiled where I had to, I got back to work so I was away from home, and at work I could be myself. I could be Natasha. At home I will always be the lady whose little girl died. I couldn't stand the sympathy and pitying looks. I know people meant well by telling me: *"God has a plan for us all"* and *"She's in a better place."* They were trying to be supportive when they said, *"Everything happens for a reason,"* and *"You're young; you can have more children."* It was torture having to smile through those well-meant sentiments. It was the last one that drove me insane, as most people did not know that I suffered with fertility issues. It had been difficult to conceive Jessica so that statement was always a kick in the gut for me.

Life moved on around me, but I was stuck. I couldn't handle the sounds of ambulance sirens. I couldn't handle the constant flashbacks, always feeling empty. I just felt completely lost. It was like the old me was trapped inside a body and looking at a face I no longer recognized. I felt different, broken, like I had died when Jessica did.

BECOMING THE LIGHT

In 2018, I hit a desperately low point and I tried to take my own life. I didn't even plan to do it but what started as a casual drink, turned into two bottles of gin and over two-hundred pills crushed into a glass and washed down in one. I awoke the next day in hospital then moved to a psychiatric hospital, and my first thought upon waking up was *why did I have to come back?*

During those hours of being out of it, I felt my soul leave my earthly body. I remember floating high above looking down at myself laying in the hospital bed. I felt no pain or sadness at leaving my body. I felt free, healthy, and whole. A tunnel of bright light appeared in front of me and I was quickly engulfed by it.

As I went into the light, I felt an overwhelming sense of peace and love. My little girl was there, she was waiting for me. I remember holding her so tight and not wanting to let go. She had grown a little, her smile and sparkling eyes still as beautiful as ever. I saw other family members, met other spiritual beings, and was shown a beautiful spiritual place which I can only describe as heaven. It felt like I had only been there a moment when a gentleman told me I had to go back. I knew I didn't have a choice. The gates of heaven were not open to me yet; it simply wasn't my time. So waking up the next evening in the hospital was super tough. It felt like losing Jessica all over again. I was crushed.

Death is not the greatest loss in life.
The greatest loss is what dies inside us while we live.

NORMAN COUSINS

When I got home, I knew I had a personality transformation. I no longer feared death. I knew my girl was ok and saw that we all live on after death. For the first time in a long time, I felt open and ready to live again—not for me, but for Jessica. I felt guided and inspired towards a new purpose in life.

Losing a loved one is a devastating blow to any family, especially your only child. Looking back in hindsight and through my own experience, I found many common attitudes and mistakes associated with death. In the western world, the subject of dying is taboo, but death is a natural part of life. I believe that our souls are eternal. The body is only a temporary vessel that allows the soul access to Earth. Karmically we are here to learn and grow.

When a person becomes more spiritually aware, they grow to understand and accept these beliefs. Looking at the two choices it should be easy to believe in life after death, rather than believe that death is final and we all have nothing else to look forward to. Losing and burying a child is something no mother should ever have to go through. But losing her showed me a different purpose and gave me a greater understanding of what more there is out there. Jessica is still here, just not in the way I want.

Every person on the planet is able to connect to spirit; it's about being open enough to receive that information, through, sound, vision, dreams, or meditation. The knowledge that there is life after death should be incorporated into all our lives, as well as the lives of your family, friends, and people who you meet along your path to eternal life. I urge you to study and become more aware of how to use this knowledge to help people who fear death. It will make their transitions happy and joyous experiences. With this knowledge they can celebrate that their loved ones are not suffering and lost forever and instead have simply migrated to a beautiful spiritual world that is filled with pure unconditional love. One day they will once again meet and be with them.

HOPE

In 2019, I set up an Instagram page: *"Natasha.Healing.The.Soul. Open."* I wanted to reach out to other grieving parents and families, to create a safe place where they could share their stories and where I could share mine without fear and judgment. It was also a place where I could share my mental health struggles to let people know they are not alone: to be honest, open, and raw.

I love helping other people—it's the way I have been all my life. It gives me a sense of joy and fulfilment. Guiding others through their loss and mental health is my main passion and also brings healing to me.

I was born with an enormous need for affection,
and a terrible need to give it.

AUDREY HEPBURN

In 2020 I started practicing my mediumship. I started soul work, meditation, and energy clearing. I'm now a fully licensed spiritual life coach, grief counselor, mindfulness and meditation coach, as well as a Master Reiki Practitioner.

Even with all I have achieved, I still struggle with mental health issues. I probably will for the rest of my life. I've come to accept that it is part of who I am.

The first six months of 2021 were really bad for me. I had fallen into a deep depression that I just couldn't get out of. I was drinking in any free time I had, eating diet pills for fun, and I had started self-harming again. I couldn't control my emotions, or impulses. I was drowning in my own mind. I was still working hard, but when alone, I was a mess. Through the constant guidance of my mentor and coach, we decided it would be a good idea for me to seek some professional help.

My general practitioner was great, she referred me back to mental health services. I started seeing the dietician team again. I also went to an eating disorder group and started AA meetings.

My new daily regime of pills was hard at first, until my body got used to them and I was put on the correct dose. In April 2021, I was diagnosed with bipolar type II. I never even knew that there were different types, but type II is usually hereditary. The hereditary aspect made a lot of sense to me as my parents have struggled emotionally, and it made me more empathetic towards them.

The turning point was a weekend away in June 2021 when everything went terribly wrong. I slipped off the no-alcohol train and ended up in hospital, with severe alcohol poisoning. It was the wake-up I needed and I haven't touched a drop since. Nor have I self-harmed and I'm off the diet pills. I am taking care of myself.

I now set boundaries by taking regular social media breaks. I also journal daily, and I write poetry sometimes, both of which gives me deep healing. I always just go with what I feel I need to write; I just write and don't think about it. I also sing, something I used to do as a child, and now it gives me peace. Before, I only ever sang for Jess or in the shower because I didn't have much confidence in myself. Since her passing, I have recorded a few songs for her and shared them publicly on her remembrance page on Facebook: *"Remembering Jessica Jean Azadi."* The page was set up by my older sister shortly after Jess passed so people could upload pictures of her—memories. It is an online place people can go to honor her.

I practice daily mantras and gratitude and I try to connect to my soul daily, work-permitting. My job as a private maternity nurse keeps me exceptionally busy, both physically and mentally. But most importantly, every day I sit and acknowledge how I am feeling and I honor those feelings by just letting them be. I still have off days where I just want to curl up in bed, but I make it out each day. I show up for me because I know I am worth it. I know I have a life worth living for and I reach out to trusted people when I'm not feeling good.

It does help, believe me.

Certain times of the year are particularly difficult: Mother's Day, her birthday, her memorial, Christmas. Every day is hard, but some days completely knock the wind out of my sails. I've found it important to acknowledge these days more and try to just be, because I know they will come and then go. I shout from the rooftops now, and embrace my true self.

Yes I have:
Bipolar II
Chronic depression
An eating disorder
Body dysmorphia
PTSD / Flashbacks
Suffer with complicated grief
Self-harming issues
Alcohol dependency issues
Diet pill addiction

However, none of these things make me a bad person: they are all a product of unhealthy coping mechanisms. These conditions do not define me. I want to show people that you can break through your own barriers and self-limitations. You can live a meaningful life, even if not a great life. Being labelled with a mental health condition does not define you.

Against all odds, with what life has thrown at me, I always manage to bounce back. Strength and resilience are two of my greatest qualities. No matter what I have been through, I know my lessons in life have only made me stronger. I've learned that bad things sometimes just happen to good people. I know I don't *"deserve"* what I have been through, but through this journey, I have found my purpose in this life. I realize that I matter, and I am worthy. I now believe that there should always be hope. Regardless of how dark things may seem, how lost you feel, you will find your way back.

And rise.

Hope is being able to see that there is
light despite all of the darkness.

DESMOND TUTU

The hardest thing to ever do is to reveal the naked soul to the world. However, in doing so brings healing, growth, strength, and powerful inspiration!

H.E. OLSEN

DR. CRAIG BEACH

Dr. Craig Beach is a Psychiatrist and the Founder and CEO of Open Mind Health—a team of mind-body-spirit experts who help people heal and thrive in the real world today. Dr. Beach is an inspiring leader, innovator, strategist, tireless mental health advocate, educator, and published author.

DOCTOR HEAL THYSELF

DR. CRAIG BEACH

*The most terrifying thing
is to accept oneself completely.*

CARL JUNG

The thing about being different is that you don't realize you are—
until you do. I was considered a *"miracle baby"* because my mother
has spina bifida, a genetic birth condition that ultimately left her
wheelchair bound. Having me was a risk to her health and life, so
I am her only child. These extraordinary circumstances and realiza-
tions have been the catalysts of my life's quest to understand, heal,
manifest, and transform.

I grew up in a very small town. As a child, my mother and
I would do household errands together. On one particularly
memorable day, my mother and I were at the mall close to home
when some random kid pointed his finger at my mother, who
was walking with a cane. *"Look at her, what's wrong with her?"* he

loudly asked his mother. I immediately bolted to hide, ending up in a department store at the other end of the mall.

My mother reacted by going to the nearby lotto booth to have her lost child paged on the loudspeaker. I must have been around ten years old at the time; I wasn't equipped to deal with the humiliation and shame I experienced in that moment, and I experienced a *"fight or flight"* reaction. I ran.

When I was thirteen years old, I was selected to be the valedictorian for my public school graduation. There was a limit of two guests per student for the ceremony. Embarrassed to be seen with my mother because of her obvious physical limitations, I gave the two tickets to my father and stepmother—even though I was closest with my mother and lived with her.

Such memories are incredibly vivid and excruciating. Yet, I also recognize that I couldn't do better at the time; I was just a kid. As an adult, I now realize that people like my mother endure experiences like this their entire lives. And one up on being "different by association" *is being different* full stop. I can't begin to imagine my mother's feelings of shame, humiliation, naked exposure, and vulnerability in such moments—and she had no option to run away like I had.

THE STRUGGLE FOR ACCEPTANCE

My parents were best friends in high school. Just as I struggled to accept my mother, my father struggled to accept both my mother and me. Even though everyone in the entire town knew my parents were married, when they would go to the grocery store my father would sometimes act as though they weren't together—intentionally hiding from her, embarrassed to be seen with her. My parents' marriage ended when I was six. These foundational experiences of shame and a struggle to accept my life reality ignited in me a laser-focused determination and hard work ethic that ultimately secured my one-way travel ticket throughout life. I graduated high school as the valedictorian and left for university on a scholarship. I didn't necessarily know where I would end up, but I knew it would be anywhere but my hometown. I now realize that I manifested it, even though I didn't realize that is what I was orchestrating at the time.

FREE TO BE ME

At age eighteen, I realized I was gay. Realizing I was different proved to be a struggle for me. I was repressed sexually; this was self-protective to avoid more shame, humiliation, and feelings of being inadequate—painful feelings that had already been imprinted as a child. As much as it's understandable and tempting to flee from your feelings and problems, it rarely works in the long run. As an *"out"* gay man now, many people have asked me, *"when did you realize you were gay?"* It sounds like such a simple question with a straightforward answer but, in my case, it isn't. Discovering I was gay was a gradual discovery process.

Interestingly, as much as I have struggled to accept my mother, she too has struggled to accept me. This realization hit me, so I waited for the *right time*—as if there is a *right time*—to tell my mom I was gay. I conveniently chose a time, four years later when we were on vacation together in Orlando, Florida.

I don't recall planning to tell her *that* night, but we had downed a bottle of Bailey's together, so it was the *"liquid courage"* that determined the timing must have been right. Buzzed, I felt more at ease and so I brought up the conversation. I wrestled with anxiety before telling her, questioning whether doing so was the right decision.

When I finally mustered up the courage—and like almost every single *"coming out"* story I have heard my entire life—my mother told me that she had suspected for a long while and that she understood and loved me. I felt such relief and reassurance in that moment. Then she added: *"just don't tell anybody at my work."*

With those seven words I realized that my mother was embarrassed of me, just as I was embarrassed of her. Like me in the mall, she too was doing the best she could in that moment. That we both did not *"fit in"* has made our mutual love deeper and stronger because we can really relate to each other. As it proves so often to be the case, raw exposure and vulnerability is a catalyst for deeper intimacy and connection. It certainly has also heightened our compassion for others.

HE LOVES ME, HE LOVES ME NOT

With my father, the connection was not as straight forward. I knew that he was very proud of me and loved me, even though he rarely told me. My father was a psychiatric nurse. He was very well respected at work, functioning more like a skilled therapist. He was notorious for his intellect, wit, charisma, and how much he helped people who were struggling emotionally. There is no doubt that my father's profession influenced my career path as I am now a psychiatrist.

Over the years I have frequently questioned my father's love for me, but I have taken some comfort in the fact that he must have loved me because I was his first child *and* we actually had the most in common. So much so, that when we worked together at the same psychiatric hospital when I returned to town for a brief period of time, one of our mutual colleagues joked about how she always wondered which Beach (the surname we shared) was walking down the hall from her office. In her opinion, we both had the identical, heavy, loud walk.

I know my father came by his parenting style and issues honestly given his own traumatic upbringing. He too did the best he could. All the same, I have experienced the negative effects of questioning my father's commitment and love for me, when such foundations are, ideally, supposed to be unwavering and unequivocal. If not adequately processed, such trauma is often contagious. For example, it has negatively impacted my ability to get close in relationships. I have struggled with intimacy; I find it difficult to feel secure and safe. This has contributed to me being, at times, overly needy, clingy, and codependent.

I have found that forgiveness is fully accepting the realities and limits of a situation or relationship and making a conscious, informed, empowered decision about what you want—or sometimes what you are capable of managing—considering the risks and benefits at play.

THE PAST IS PRESENT

My parents both remarried and I have two half-brothers and an adopted sister through my father. This type of childhood chaos and inconsistency left me, on one hand, frantic for stability, love, and security and, on the other hand, not feeling like I could trust anyone. When the love felt good, I ended up clingy and desperate for it. When the love was questionable or unstable, I was detached, aloof, cold—all of which serves to self-protect.

Perhaps not unlike many children of divorce, I have worked hard to do better than my parents did by having more stable intimate relationships. To be honest, my pattern would probably best be described as a serial monogamist. I know that my traumatic background has made it difficult for me to get close to people intimately, including sexually. Despite several rounds of therapy, I have residual intimacy issues. I do feel very grateful that I have had several opportunities to marry over the years. I was engaged once and close to marrying, but that relationship didn't work. I later ended up marrying, but that also hasn't stood the test of time. I recently divorced my partner of eight years. We were married for four-and-a-half of them.

I'm not sure why I ever thought I would be good at marriage. I didn't have any good role models growing up. From my perspective, I feel my marriage ended because we were two different people who couldn't ultimately accept and embrace each other sufficiently to make things work.

BREAKTHROUGHS

Out of life's school of war:
What does not destroy me,
Makes me stronger.

FRIEDRICH NIETZSCHE

I have come to learn that I have not only persisted despite adversity and trauma, but I'm stronger and better *because* of it. To me, it's very healing to know that I'm a better version of myself, and I have realized greater potential having experienced these hardships than if I had an easier life. I know that the adversity has positively influenced my character development and has allowed me to be a more genuine, real, and relatable person who comes by compassion naturally. These traits likely would not be as pronounced had my background been more of a cakewalk.

Over the years, I have translated shame and humiliation into pride in my strength and tenacity. I have found time and time again that when I risked being vulnerable and open with others, *that* encouraged others to risk the same. And doesn't deep intimacy derive from shared vulnerability and risk-taking?

Some would see the risks I have experienced and taken in my life as daunting, but this has helped me become more comfortable with the uncomfortable, embrace risk, and even be exhilarated by uncertainty. One of my best friends jokes that I have a *"shockingly high tolerance for risk."* I did not even grasp what she meant, but I now take this as a compliment. I know that comfort with risk has allowed me to move on from people, jobs, and situations which haven't served me well—as scary as it has sometimes been. I accept what I cannot change, but I don't allow myself to settle or stagnate. I no longer move on with bitterness and resentment. And to me, that *is* true forgiveness.

I view my life as a series of small successive miracles that literally commenced the day I was born. Life isn't random or accidental; we are all the conductors of the magic we make of our lives. I am no victim, although many have viewed me as one over the years. Rather, I am an empowered manifester of my magnificence.

EMBRACING AUTHENTICITY

To thine own self be true,
and it must follow, as the night the day,
thou canst not then be false to any man.

WILLIAM SHAKESPEARE

Much of what I have learned over the years, and the associated transformations I am describing, require a fundamental mindset shift. We must commit to a life of joy, play, music, and abundance versus a fear-based and scarcity mentality—the ones so many of us live. Our fear is conditioned, and we are often on autopilot; we aren't even aware that different and better *is* possible. It doesn't need to hurt *that bad!* What is important is to not merely accept the status quo—mediocrity—and settle in. This is what I view as the easy way. True happiness derives from doing what's right, not what's easy.

As an adult, that growth mindset has allowed me to realize my purpose and find meaning. It has permitted me to move on from relationships of all types that weren't working or a good fit. It has pushed me to pivot from more safe, traditional jobs towards greater freedom and creative professional pursuits where I have more opportunity and power to realize both my true potential and mission. It is this extension from my comfort zone where my joy and contributions are endless.

I have learned that being different is really a gift and its rewards include having a potentially easier pathway to becoming a truly authentic person. You become more comfortable in your own skin because you are seasoned at it. You don't phase easily because you have been to many rodeos. You don't realize it while in motion, but you are harnessing psychological resiliency—life's armor.

Trauma is a powerful teacher. Even when many things fail, it is often for good reasons. I have learned that my mindset and perspective are critical to how I view the world, how I show up, and where I end up. The adage of glass half full versus half empty is really a gratitude mindset. It takes a lot of work to become more open to embracing adversity, trauma, and hardship for the hard lessons that create strength, character, and tenacity.

My life hasn't been one where opportunities have always been thrown at me, or where things were even easily available. But this, too, has forced me to create new options and exciting possibilities for growth. I have thrived from embracing a mindset of radically accepting what is—however unpleasant and painful it may be— and I have found taking full responsibility and accountability to be essential to my own healing.

Often, it's not about becoming a new person,
but becoming the person you were meant to be,
and already are, but don't know how to be.

HEATH L. BUCKMASTE

As I began to love myself I found that anguish and emotional suffering are only warning signs that I was living against my own truth. Today, I know this is 'authenticity.'

CHARLIE CHAPLIN

LISA CARTER

Lisa Carter is a published author, Reiki Master, certified Life Coach, and has added Real Estate Agent to her professional credentials. After twenty-eight years, she left her corporate career behind. Her life is the epitome of GRIT. She's been from hell and back and is a thriver. Lisa is passionate about helping others and making a difference.

UNBREAKABLE

LISA CARTER

The human capacity for burden is like bamboo—
far more flexible than you'd ever believe at first glance.

JODI PICOULT

Being the firstborn in my family, I was spoiled and loved. My parents and grandparents doted on me, treating me like I was special, as I was their *"only"*—my brother came six years later. However, it was also an unhappy and dysfunctional home with an alcoholic father. My mother was overwhelmed and struggled to cope with the chaos his addiction caused.

To help *me* cope, I had to find *someone* who would understand; someone I could talk to and didn't have to share with anyone else. I asked for it and there she was... my *guardian angel*. From my earliest memories, she and I talked every night before I went to sleep. Throughout my life, even though it felt like she was nowhere to be found, I now know that she had always been by my side.

We often think that we are alone, particularly in times of extreme chaos. The clarity is knowing that whatever we have gone through is happening *for* us, not against us. Chaos seemed to be my middle name. We make choices based on how we feel about ourselves.

SCHOOL OF HARD KNOCKS

One of my first choices was to quit school in tenth grade. In hindsight, I know it wasn't the smartest decision, but I couldn't study or pay attention. I felt like I didn't belong there. This was the time I dabbled in some teenager shenanigans: I stole once (got caught), smoked pot, drank, and snuck out of the house at night, but none of this behavior felt like me either. This was not what I wanted for myself. My little inner voice and my gut told me that this is not who I was, or perhaps it was my guardian angel nudging at me, telling me I was destined for something greater. I regretted quitting school, so I went back. Education is an important part of my journey, both through formal courses and the school of hard knocks.

When I was eighteen, my mother left my father because she couldn't take it anymore. I don't blame her: she'd had her share of pain. But, after my mom moved out of our house, I ended up taking over her responsibilities. Groceries, laundry, cleaning, cooking all just to keep the peace. I thought maybe with my mom gone, my father would come to his senses; however, that never happened.

SABOTAGE

I met the man I thought would be my forever when I was eighteen and we bought a house together a year later. He wanted to spend time with me all the time; I thought, *wow, he must really like me*. If I made plans with my girlfriends, or other groups of friends, he would always find something for us to do to convince me to cancel and be with him instead. Back then, I thought he must care so much. Now I see an entirely different picture—he was a classic narcissist.

We moved into our house and brought my grandfather to live with us because he was alone. After a year, I decided I wanted to go back to school to get my GED. Over the next few months, I saw a completely different side of this man I moved in with. I had seen flashes of it before as he was a drinker, but coming from an alcoholic home, this appeared normal to me.

After a few months of being a student, Max made it difficult for me to attend school. Looking back now, I realize it was because he didn't want me to do anything that would give me strength. He did everything he could to put me down, to make himself feel superior to me. Max needed to think he had saved a poor damsel in distress, rescued me from an alcoholic home, and was a hero, ready to take care of me. Thus, he resisted any of my attempts to become more empowered. I realized there was no difference between him and my dad. They were both drinkers. However, unlike my dad, he was both physically and mentally abusive.

I got up one morning and started packing to leave. *Hell, if I was going to live with an alcoholic, I might as well go back home*, I thought to myself. However, my father's house had become

31

a party house. With my mom gone, my father drank more than ever and did not prevent my teenage brother from having all his friends in and out of the house. Some of his friends even lived there. There was no chance of me going back now. Max begged me to stay and promised he would quit drinking, which he did.

We decided to get married the following April. I found out two months before our wedding date that I was pregnant with my son. Plus, Max was drinking again. Things were not great, but I tried my best to make things work because I had nowhere else to go, especially with a baby and my grandfather in tow.

I continued to have this strong desire to make more of myself and continually looked for opportunities. I had two more children with Max, even though I always knew I wouldn't be with him forever, or even for a long time. I never once made plans or talked about our future as I somehow knew he wouldn't be in it; I continued to enrol in courses despite his efforts to stop me. Just like the previous time I went to school, he would try to control the situation on class nights. He would show up late, or not at all, making me miss classes. I knew I had to do more for myself and for my three children, who were all under the age of five. Besides the classes, I worked part time in the evenings and babysat a few children during the day to make my own money.

The night of my exam, I didn't have a babysitter available. Max promised he would be home. I spoke to him as he was leaving his office to come home. He never showed up. Not only did he not show up that night, he didn't arrive home until after noon the next day. I had missed my exam. Everything I tried to do to better myself, he sabotaged. I never went back to classes.

SILENCE, ABUSED AND TRAPPED

Over the next couple of years, it was worse than ever. I could not predict whether he would come home drunk or what kind of night was in store. I would kick him out to his mom's house about every three to four months. He would stay there for a few days until things blew over. I felt so strapped and trapped.

Soon, the abuse hit an all-time high. I had three kids, no actual income, and still no education. I felt like every time I tried to move forward, he would block me. I never talked about the abuse, only two close friends knew. I'm still unsure if I was embarrassed that I allowed this to happen to me, or if, deep down, I thought I deserved it.

I felt like an imposter. On the outside, I looked like a mom and wife with a perfect little life, but on this inside, I was suffering. My house was spotless. Laundry always done, cut the grass, did the gardening, vacuumed the pool. I did everything plus more. I was obsessed. Basically, I spent years controlling all the things I could because I couldn't control my own safety.

I kept searching and praying, trying to find the answers. My guardian angel felt so far away; all I had in front of me was a dark blank space. *Why weren't the answers coming easily to me? Why was I living this abusive nightmare? What did I do to deserve this? How do I get out of this mess? Where was she when I need her to most?* I had never felt so alone.

After another terrible, abusive night, I knew I had to do something. I sat with my friend, and we made an escape plan. Solid plan, right? I lasted a month.

FINAL STRAW

A few days after the New Year, I took the kids out for the day by myself, as Max had something more important to do… *drink*. When I got home, he wasn't there. I began making dinner and got the kids settled with a movie.

Max stumbled in, so intoxicated that he could barely stand. And yes: he drove home like that. I could tell by the first words out of his mouth what kind of night was ahead. He was looking for a fight. I did my best to stay out of his way and keep the kids occupied and quiet. I should have just called the police, just like I should have a thousand times before, but never did. He would most likely still be in jail if I had.

I went upstairs to get my three-year-old ready for bath time and bed. Max followed me and stood waiting for me at the top of the stairs as I approached them from the bathroom. With my daughter in my arms, he was primed for a fight. He said, *"go ahead, try to go down and I will kick you down the stairs."* I told him I was holding *his* daughter. *"What's wrong with you?"* I said. But he wasn't really seeing the situation, as he was hell-bent on hurting me. He was on a mission, and I was his target.

He was standing, staggering—trying to get his balance. I quickly passed him and headed down the stairs. It was at the very moment something came over me: an inner strength I had not felt before. *Not like this*, I thought. You can hurt me and threaten me, but he had just crossed a line. He threatened one of my children. He followed me down the stairs and, mercifully, continued to the basement where he thankfully passed out, but not before yelling, *"don't close your eyes tonight because tonight is the night you are going to die!"*

The next morning when he woke up from the couch in the basement, where he often slept, I handed him a coffee, and just smiled. He had a very confused look on his face. I could see him scrambling, trying to remember the night before, but I just sat there and didn't say a word. As he got up, he cautiously took the coffee, still looking very puzzled with, I am sure, mere flashes of the night before going through his head.

Still smiling, I told him he was leaving and now I was calling the shots. I outlined exactly how things were going to happen. I told him I'd needed one year to get myself organized. He would continue paying the bills, see the kids only at his mother's house on weekends, and that he was no longer coming back. I knew deep down that I wasn't alone: my guardian angel was back. She was right beside me. I felt so empowered.

FALLING INTO PLACE

Here I was a month after turning thirty: a single mom with three kids—aged eight, six, and three-and-a-half—and my grandfather. I had no clue what to do next, but I had a year to figure it all out. One step at a time. The first big step was now behind me.

The matrimonial house sold after a few months, and I had to find another place for us to live. Max tried to control the situation by not signing the separation papers and tying up the money from the house, so I couldn't buy a house. I was looking for rentals, but there wasn't much available. With literally twelve days until move date, and pressure from my lawyer, he finally signed the separation papers. I had eleven days to pack, find a home, a mortgage, and movers. Once again, survival mode kicked in. Everything

I needed completely fell into place. I was literally guided through every step of the process. The house I purchased had been vacant for over eighteen months and desperately needed far more than TLC. In fact, it was a complete disaster, but it had four bedrooms, a backyard, was owned by the bank, and we could close on time. What really sold me on this house was the three little duck hooks in the hall closet. It was a sign. I knew that this was my new home.

Once we moved in, I had ten days before school started to arrange daycare for my youngest, and an after school program for my other two. I should have been more concerned, but somehow, I just knew it would turn out. While I was registering at the school, I met Jean by accident. I say by accident because I wasn't supposed to be there at that time of day; I mixed up my appointment time. Jean lived around the corner, almost directly behind me. We started talking and to my surprise (maybe not) she did daycare and had spots for my kids. Everything was falling perfectly into place.

HE WILL NOT WIN

Almost a year to date, coming home from back-to-school shopping with the kids, I pulled into the driveway and had this very funny feeling. Something was wrong, very wrong. When I went in the house, the kids went to watch TV and I headed up to have a shower. My grandfather's room was quiet, no TV on. This was unusual. I had a horrible feeling at this point. I knocked on his door. No answer. I took a deep breath as I opened the door, afraid of what I might see. There he was, lying on the floor with both his hands resting on his chest. He was gone. He'd had a heart attack.

Ten months later, my dad had surgery on his back. He had the same operation the year before, but his heart stopped beating during the procedure. They revived him, but decided it was too risky to continue the surgery. He was in so much pain he had no other option but to go back for the same surgery. My dad kept telling me he would not make it through this surgery and was putting things in place in the event he was right. I wouldn't listen; I told him that was crazy. He made it through the surgery, but he died ten days later due to complications, the fault of the hospital.

During this time, which should have been spent grieving, Max was still doing everything he could to make my life a living hell. In his mind, this second loss would make me go running back to him. Instead, it gave me more motivation to succeed. However, Max made it his mission to keep fueling the fire. Every week there was something new. At one point, he spent months hiding all his assets in other people's names and took me back to court to get child support reduced. His lawyer claimed he was struggling; he had no job (not on record anyway) and had no assets. The courts bought it. After all, I had a house, a full-time job, and was raising three children. They reduced child support to the equivalent of half a month's groceries.

My entire world was crumbling because of the stress of losing both my grandfather and my dad in such a short period of each other *and* the divorce. At times I would ask myself, *How am I going to keep myself together?* The answer fuelled me and made me even stronger. My mantra became *"he will not win."*

Max was relentless. He continued to harass me to the point the police were involved. He was eventually charged with damaging my property and trespassing. That still didn't stop him.

One night, in a rage, he told someone he was on his way to kill me. He had written a letter detailing how I was going to die. It said that he was *"going to slit my throat from one side to the other, then burn down my house."* When Max got in his car and left, the person he told called the police. I arrived home from work, and within an hour, my house was surrounded by five police cruisers and a SWAT van. Police with guns surrounded my house looking for him. A cruiser stayed to watch over me until Max was arrested a few hours later. They found a can of gasoline and a large knife in his car.

STEPPING INTO MY POWER

Angels assist us in connecting
with a powerful yet gentle force,
which encourages us
to live life to its fullest.

DENISE LINN

Enough was enough. I needed to take things into my own hands, and I had a plan. I was going to summarize the past four years of his actions for the judge: the lies, the hidden assets, the income he had hidden, all the police charges, confirmation he had not paid child support, and whatever else I could find. I needed him gone.

My guardian angels were right there with me. I believe I was being guided throughout the entire plan. I would think things and they would appear. I would close my eyes at night and have the answers. Things came to me with very little effort. Within a short time, I had everything I needed. I then hired a lawyer to discuss next steps.

The lawyer suggested I represent myself. She would help me prep and guide me on what to do, but I would be the one standing up in court, representing myself and arguing my case against his lawyer and directly to the judge. My ask to the courts was for him to pay a onetime lump sum of money (basically covered back child support) and that all access and visitation to the kids be removed.

I won. The judge thanked me for coming into her court so well prepared, and more prepared than most lawyers that stand in front of her. She said, *"you should be very proud of yourself today."*

I was very proud of myself. It was a double win.

CANCER? ARE YOU KIDDING ME?

Yet the hits kept coming. About ten years later, all within a two-year period, I was diagnosed with thyroid cancer, lost my job of fourteen years, had to sell my home, and I had to apply for debt consolidation.

Over that time, dealing with cancer and its treatment, including trying to find the correct balance of medication, I also found myself tossed directly into full-on menopause. To say I was exhausted would be an understatement, yet somehow I knew I was going to be ok. It gave me so much time to reflect on where I needed to make changes in my life and dig deeper into my spirituality. Having previously studied Reiki, I immersed myself in this practice to help me heal mind, body, and soul. I also started meditation, daily walks, and changing my daily habits. Even after all this, I knew that there was a bigger plan for me. I had questions, and didn't know how, but I had a powerful belief and knowing that I was going to be ok. I was resilient. I bent but didn't break. I believed I was being spiritually guided. I summoned up my strength and guardian angel. I consolidated my debt, got a new car, and a new job—a better job.

Things ended up taking a turn again in the next few years, as my bad habits were slowing creeping back. My job was so busy that I no longer took time out for me. I rarely attended meditation classes, nor did I practice my Reiki.

During one of my regular checkups, my endocrinologist found another nodule in my neck. I had no thyroid, so this time it was most likely on my lymphoid. I was booked in for an ultrasound and the tests came back positive. The doctor booked me to go back in a few months so they could monitor it. This was my wake-up call. I did some deep reflection and meditating. I saw I was falling back into the same chaos I had once lived and that this was no longer my journey. I immediately started making changes to find balance, getting back to my Reiki, meditation, and good daily habits of putting me first and not taking on more chaos.

Months later, when I attended my follow-up ultrasound, they couldn't find the nodule. They called in another doctor, then the specialist, as somehow, mysteriously, it was gone. I knew deep down that this was a warning, and once again I was being redirected to the path I was meant to walk on and that I was not going back.

I truly believe that I am exactly where I am meant to be, and that all that has happened in my life has happened *for* me, not *to* me. My journey has left me stronger and more resilient. Today I live to thrive, not just survive. I *am* unbreakable.

Your history doesn't define you; it creates you.

DANIEL ABBOTT

There are wounds that never show on

the body that are deeper and more

hurtful than anything that bleeds.

LAURELL K. HAMILTON

KIM MURPHY

Kim Murphy is a published author and certified Master Empowerment Coach. Her journey has taken her on a rollercoaster ride to get to where she was truly meant to be. Through the process, she was able to heal her old wounds and believe in herself. Kim believes that it is never too late to transform your life. Her passion is to help other women globally do the same. Kim enjoys spending time with her children and grandchildren and currently lives in Ontario, Canada.

THE ROAD TO BECOMING

KIM MURPHY

Take the road less traveled.
Get lost if you must,
because only in losing yourself
will you find your true path.

VIRGINIA ALISON

As a child who was raised in a toxic, unhappy home, I have always struggled with finding my voice and myself. My three brothers and I were raised to believe that *"children should be seen and not heard."* Oddly enough, this mantra we had did not affect my brothers, but it hit me hard. As a natural born extrovert, this silence did not bode well with my personality. Always the chatter-box, it became clear it was not safe to speak; the repercussions were too severe. I was squashed into submissiveness by my mother's guilt and shame, which hurt me more than any spanking ever could. These emotional scars have lasted a lifetime.

All I wanted was love, compassion, and approval from my mother, which was nowhere to be found. Expressing my emotions was also frowned upon. Shedding tears of sadness, unhappiness or fear, all natural reactions for a child, was unacceptable and were met with *"stop crying or I will give you something to cry for!"*

Those *"little things"* I craved, like support and physical hugs, were met with disdain and disapproval. The constant rebuffs had me continually shrinking into a smaller place. I pretended everything was okay while living with the confusion about what I had done wrong and why I wasn't loved. I tried seeking approval from my mother, but sadly, she herself was too broken to understand anyone else's needs, especially those of her children. I was *"the good girl"* and helped my mother, figuring this would make her happy and therefore love me. Unfortunately, there was never any rhyme or reason to it—she just spewed wrath and anger. To cope, at the age of eight, I ended up turning to food for comfort and solace, which became a lifelong battle.

I became a people pleaser, doing whatever I could to make others happy, often at my expense. At the age of ten, I was out price shopping and buying the groceries for our family. When I was finished the shopping, I would call my father to pick me up at the grocery store. My mother had worked full-time *and* took care of the house and children, so she delegated all of the household chores to me. I learned to cook and clean, but our house was always a mess because I couldn't keep up with my brothers. I often questioned why I had to do all the cooking, cleaning and laundry while my brothers played, but there never was a straightforward answer or change. This servitude instilled resentment within me.

My parents divorced when I was thirteen, unusual in the 1970s. Since my mother seemingly needed someone to argue with, it was me who took the brunt of it. Blame was one of her weapons. After every argument, there would be a note on my dresser, blaming me and wondering what caused *me* to be so harsh. It was always my fault.

As an escape, I began hiding at friends' houses. Oh, the love and joy these families had was such a mystery to me. Their parents were strict, but they weren't cruel, so I spent as many evenings as I could there because I felt free.

THINGS CHANGE BUT STAY THE SAME

As a teenager, in my search for love, I thought boys would fill the void. At the age of fifteen, I met my future husband. He was kind, funny and generous. Best of all, he came from a family that had Sunday dinners together. He was a good man, but the icing on the cake for me was his mother. How I adored her. She talked to me, taught me to cook, showed me kindness and love. I was in hook-line and sinker. We were married nine days after I turned twenty.

To fit into my new marriage and family, I had to become someone I wasn't. I had hoped my new life would allow me to escape my childhood history of feeling alone and unloved. A few years into my marriage, I realized I still had no voice, felt no genuine love and still felt empty inside. I did what my husband and new family expected of me. I was devoted to them and did whatever would gain the approval of my husband and mother-in-law. I didn't even go to college until I had my mother-in-law's approval first. She ruled the roost; my husband's opinion came in second.

As life went on, I continued to simmer in resentment for not getting my needs met, feeling alone and leading a life of always being expected to be everything to everyone. Family was important to me and I did look forward to spending quality time with our three beautiful children. That kept me going as I relished in the endless hours I spent taking them to their after school activities. I scrimped and saved because that was what my husband wanted. I felt invisible and lost my identity. I had become a wife, the mom and Kim from Computer Services at my job. Kim, the wonderful, kind, loving woman was what I showed on the outside, but not how I felt within myself. I was still lost and hiding my true self.

After a few years of marriage and suffering in silence, I displayed a similar destructive pattern of rage and anger that my mother exhibited. I had an incident with my sister-in-law and told her off like nobody's business. I went up one side of her and down the other. I was clearly out of line—the anger I had brewing because of my unhappiness was not my sister-in-law's fault, but she got it none-the-less.

My anger was costly. I didn't realize the full impact until my beloved mother-in-law stopped speaking to me because of my outburst. Blood is thicker than a marriage license. Looking back at it, I realize this was the start of many occasions where my unhappiness reared its ugly head with self-sabotage. I grew up believing I did not deserve love or happiness; a loving family certainly was not in my deserve level and I subconsciously destroyed the relationship.

FINDING MY VOICE

It took me quite a long time to develop a voice,
and now that I have it, I am not going to be silent.

MADELEINE K. ALBRIGHT

I was now truly isolated in my marriage; my extended in-law family was gone. I buried myself in my children and my work. I paid the bills, saved money, took care of the household—all the things my husband expected of me. Saving money was most important of all; he seemed to value money more than he did me. As I saved, I would say yes to whatever he wanted to make him happy. I did have one ask, however: that on our tenth wedding anniversary we go away to Dominican Republic. Silly me, I assumed his silence was acceptance of my one request. For ten years we went on. I tried to be happy, but I felt so empty.

As our tenth anniversary approached, I mentioned to my husband that we should start looking into our trip. I was hit right between the eyes by his statement *"I am not wasting money on a trip with you!"* Something inside me snapped, *"what the heck was I doing?"* I married him to be part of a family that was now gone. I married to be in a team with my husband and have kids. All of this time I did whatever *he* wanted, at the expense of my self-worth and self-esteem and he just shut me down completely with my *one* ask!

This incident caused a huge awakening within me. My thoughts went to *"What about me!?"* I felt I couldn't be all-in with a marriage that continued to be one-sided. Funny how once you have that

47

proverbial straw broken, you just can't go back. My silence was now broken. I started to speak up and have opinions. My husband didn't know how to deal with that at all so, the fighting began. When I stood up for myself, he would then end arguments by saying, *"fine, we should separate."* I knew this was just to shut me up and at first I wasn't ready to separate. Finally, though, I grabbed that separation ball and ran with it. I was fed up being married to a man that didn't appreciate me, for me.

SELF-DESTRUCTION

Relieved to be on my own, I believed things were going to be different. I knew I had to *"figure myself out"* before I could move forward with a new independent life. Sadly, because of the years of pent-up resentment, my anger bubbled to the surface, and it presented itself in very counter-intuitive ways. I don't even have a mean streak, but I was so used to not expressing myself that I went overboard. I would happily tell off whoever ticked me off, both harshly and unfiltered.

I didn't feel that I deserved love or happiness, so this spewing of anger was a subconscious sabotage to keep everyone at a distance. For the better part of ten years, I created self-destructive patterns of behavior. If something was going well, somehow, some way, I made sure it stopped. Financially, I was close to ruin so many times. Living with a "lack" mindset was in my comfort zone. Success and wealth didn't feel comfortable because I felt I wasn't worthy of it. It became a vicious cycle. My negative self-talk would also contribute to my demise. It was like a self-fulfilled prophecy. I created ruin and chaos around me, but then I also had enough to fight in me to bounce back. I would find a good job, get downsized, start a business only to fail, then get a better job only to be downsized again and start another business, to fail. I kept repeating these destructive patterns, validating my lack of self-worth.

CRASH AND BURN

I had my first crash-and-burn in my forties. People recognized it and told me I was suffering from depression. I refused to believe them. My denial, of course, was part of the issue.

Christmas had always been a very busy and disappointing time for me. I took care of everyone else: making sure they were happy, gifts wrapped, cookies baked, and dinner included all the favorite dishes. When it was all done, the kids went to their father's house and I was filled with a deep emptiness.

On this particular Christmas, my depression really hit me. As usual, I had done too much and was exhausted. After the kids left to visit their father's house, I sat down for a moment to catch my breath. My brain was swirling with all the things on my to-do list, but I just couldn't move. I could finally get up, shower, and put on the new pyjamas Santa brought me. After putting the turkey in the oven, I sat down again. I intrinsically knew there was something wrong because I couldn't bring myself to get up off the couch. I literally sat there for four hours until the kids came home.

When my children arrived, I jumped up and pretended everything was fine; kicking *"super mom"* into high gear. We had our lovely Christmas dinner and I hid my issue from them. I never shared what was going on with me to anybody, always pretending that everything was going well. However, I was very concerned because I mentioned what happened to me to a colleague at work. She recommended I see a psychologist and a naturopath.

After our meeting, the psychologist concluded I was fine. *Whew!* I received a clean bill of health and dodged an *official* diagnosis of depression. The naturopath said that I was exhausted from adrenal fatigue. That made sense to me, a single working mom with three serious athletes for children and constantly running all over the place with them. She gave me supplements to take, but they really didn't resolve my exhaustion, mood, or self-sabotaging behavior.

The crash opened my eyes to looking into the bigger picture and further discovering and understanding myself. It put me on a path of self-help and personal development. I started taking courses, tried to honor and focus positively on myself, and I discovered coaching. I loved coaching and felt that it was my true calling. However, my emotional self-harm and self-loathing were so deeply rooted within me that I was never truly successful in launching and sustaining my business. I realized I wasn't ready and still had more work to do on myself. So I went back to getting a job, to only be downsized again. The pattern continued.

Although I delved deeper within myself, I was still in denial and unaware of what my destructive patterns truly were. Even though mental health issues are prevalent on both sides of my family, there was no way it could hit me, I thought, as I am too strong! Looking back, I now realize that I actively made sure I would fail because of my fear of success and happiness.

The men I dated after my divorce also fed into my lack of self-worth. I attracted men who needed to be taken care of and wanted someone to mother them. That was my jam! But my anger and resentment of taking care of everyone else never allowed me to have a long-term relationship. I always found an excuse to end it. Every road I took lead me to self-loathing. I appeared happy on the outside, but inside I was a mess.

SAVING MYSELF

My last crash happened and I hit my ultimate rock bottom. I had floundered for a few more years, then I lost both my house and then my apartment. Close to being homeless, my daughter stepped in and had me move in with her to help care for my grandson when she worked shifts. I felt I was pathetic, disconnected, unhappy, and emotionally depleted.

I was sinking into the depths of disdain and self-pity. Logically, all I had to do was stand up and take care of myself. Easier said than done—I felt I couldn't muster up the strength. As the casualty of my self-sabotage, I felt so helpless. I was conflicted with that because asking for help went against the grain of all my personal values as a strong independent woman, yet I was in such despair that was my only thought: *Who will save me?*

Searching for answers, I found an empowerment course, which was the lifeline I needed. It was a three-month telecourse that literally changed the trajectory of my life. For the first time in a very long time, I felt ignited and ready to start standing up for myself and seeing my worth. I had to go deep, take it one step at a time to heal those old scars to understand that I am worthy of love and happiness. I came to understand that I wasn't alone and that I could ask for help. It was actually liberating to do so.

As a habitual people pleaser, I did not know that help was even an option for me.

My focused healing began and continued slowly. Learning to love and accept myself—mind, body, and soul—was so foreign to me. A big revelation for me was I needed to come to terms with the fact that although the trauma I was raised with wasn't my fault, I didn't need to be a victim. I had the power to change. I know that I have overcome so much of my deep-seated trauma and have embraced the neglected little girl I was by loving and nurturing *her*, my beautiful inner child. Self-forgiveness for who she was has also been such a powerful transformation, and is instrumental in my healing, as well as in my forgiveness of others. I no longer harbor anger and resentment.

Knowing that I had the power within me and my love for coaching, I graduated from both the Personal Empowerment Certification and Master Empowerment Certification. We are each an ever evolving work in progress. I have turned my passion for coaching into helping other women overcome their own limiting beliefs so they may become the powerful women they are meant to be.

One of my favorite lines from my empowerment coaching program is that *"we are captains of our own ship."* For me this means we have to realize that no matter what anyone else says, we are enough. I coached myself through my limiting beliefs and now I coach women that we don't need anyone else to *"save us."* We each have the ability to save ourselves when we dig deep and do the work. In order for us to become who *we will be*, we have to be ready to surrender our preconceived ideas about ourselves and relearn who we truly *are*.

With all the twists and turns, the road to becoming my best self has been a long and rewarding one. Gone are the limiting beliefs of feeling less than. Learning to lean into my emotions and express them has been life changing. I am unapologetically me to stand in my power with love for myself. I realize it was within me all along. My path has given me the gift of a powerful voice, strong yet refined. I no longer feel lost and alone searching for myself. I found *her*; I inherently know that *she* is worthy and lovable.

You've always had the power, my dear,
You just had to learn it for yourself.

GLINDA, THE GOOD WITCH
THE WIZARD OF OZ

Self-love can only be achieved by living
an authentic life. It's not possible to
truly love and accept yourself when
you are not being true to yourself.

ANTHON ST. MAARTEN

MARTIN REID

Martin Reid is an entrepreneur who left the corporate world in 2017 to start Reid's Gin Distillery in Toronto with his three kids. An accomplished executive in Financial Services, Martin understands the value of living life to its fullest. Leaving the corporate world once before in 2001, he took his family sailing for two years through the Caribbean, Venezuela and the East Coast of North America. Martin currently lives in Toronto.

A FACTORY WORKER'S SON

MARTIN REID

You can choose courage
or you can choose comfort.
You can't have both.

BRENÉ BROWN

Growing up we struggled with five of us living in a two-bedroom basement apartment. My brother and I were in one bedroom and my parents were in the other. A curtain was hung between the living and dining room and my sister had the dining room as her bedroom. It was a simple upbringing and although both my parents worked very hard, they barely got by financially.

It bothered me that life was hard for my parents. I also noticed how poor we seemed to be compared to other kids, not that I was wanting for anything. I remember my parents were given a queen size mattress from my aunt and uncle, but we needed twin mattresses. So, to make do, my parents cut the mattress in two, springs and all, then sewed the edges back up to give my brother and I a new twin mattress each.

My dad often worked shifts and seven days a week to try to get a little further ahead. Both my parents emigrated from the UK to Canada; they brought with them their very British working-class mindset. My parents accepted their situation, tried to work within it, and did the best they could. They didn't think it was possible to do more. My father would often tell me as a matter of fact, *"you will always be a factory worker's son."* He believed that would be my lot in life, too. This is how he viewed things. I was determined to prove him wrong and not to settle. My mother on the other hand, always said, *"you can do anything you want, if you really want to."*

As a kid, I read a lot about successful entrepreneurs. It opened my eyes to what was possible and could be. I was determined to change my future, and do more than my parents' could, but it was going to push me out of my comfort zone. It would require me to take those chances by myself. First off, I would need to go to university which was something new in the Reid family.

I really had to force myself to go outside of my comfort zone. Often, I played it safe, and didn't take many chances, never venturing too far out from a safe place to avoid exposing myself to unnecessary risk as going outside of my comfort zone was terrifying to me. Being an introvert, I quietly did my thing hoping nobody would notice. The fear of failure, particularly the fear of making a fool of myself, kept me in a safe place. I would visualize every possible scenario so that I could be prepared for whatever outcome happened. I never wanted to look like I was *"not in control."*

My parents questioned my decision to go to university. At the time, there were job opportunities that offered good money and they felt that I was going to miss out. In the end they supported me in my choice, but they didn't understand it. My dad had dropped out of school at fourteen years old and he didn't understand why I wouldn't do the same and make money as soon as I could. Even the student counselor at high school thought I was wasting my time going to university. I was determined to prove them *all* wrong. I wanted them to see that not only I could do it, but also that it was worth it. When I completed my university degree, my parents were there at my graduation and were very proud. That meant the world to me.

PLAYING SAFE NO MORE

Towards the end of university, I met Julie who had just returned from a year studying in Europe. She had a confidence about trying new things that I couldn't fathom. Julie took chances that I only dreamed of. We got engaged and after university, we backpacked around the world for a year pushing ourselves out of our comfort zones. Before meeting her, I would never have even thought I would have traveled so far, but with her, taking the risk wasn't as frightening and there we were backpacking around the world. She taught me that it was ok to fail, that the rewards were well worth it.

No longer was I afraid of failing and playing it safe. In fact, as I pushed myself out of my comfort zone and accomplished some of my dreams, I grew more confident about taking chances. I still worried about not appearing to be in control and continued to visualize the outcomes so that I could be prepared. That fear of failure didn't limit me; instead it pushed me. The more I got out of my comfort zone and succeeded the more I was willing to push the limits, whether running a marathon or jumping out of a plane at 13,000 feet. The quiet boy who played it safe was replaced by a young man who was willing to quietly push his boundaries and was proud of many of the accomplishments in his life.

It was that confidence that allowed me to take risks with my career. To further my career and realize my dream, I relocated with my wife and three kids to New York. The courage to take on the role of company president later on in my career, required me to push the limits of my comfort even more as I took on a more public role. I was always the kid in school who would never put his hand up. I hated public speaking and here I was speaking in front of thousands of people or going on TV. I was scared, but it didn't paralyze me. It didn't stop me from accomplishing my goals.

LIFE IS TOO SHORT

Within a two-year period, I lost my job of eighteen years and *both* my parents. I felt like I had been beaten up.

The death of my parents left a big hole that couldn't be filled. They were both so young—my dad seventy-one and my mother sixty-six. They had worked so hard their entire lives and enjoyed retirement for only a short while. It didn't seem fair. It bothered me that after all their work, they did not get much of a chance to enjoy life. My mother always wanted to dance at her grand-children's wedding. That wasn't going to happen. A lot of things weren't going to happen. I wanted to show them that I wasn't *"just a factory worker's son"* and didn't have to be limited by that. I had wanted them to see my success and to share it with them. I became even more determined to push beyond my comfort zone and do the things I wanted to do. I came to the realization that life was too short and to appreciate living in the present.

TACKLING THE SEAS

Julie and I decided to sell everything, pull the kids out of school, and take off on a sailboat for two years. The boat trip was a massive undertaking and was well beyond the scope of anything else we had ever done. At the beginning of planning it, we weren't as scared and nervous as all our friends and families were. We just worked through things logically. It wasn't until we were getting ready to leave the dock that I think we were really scared.

The day we left was one of the most terrifying moments of my life. *What was I doing? Why am I doing this?* I thought to myself. *What's wrong with the comfortable life that we have?* A million things were running through my mind. Although I was frightened, and questioned myself, it felt like the right thing to do, and we forged ahead with our plans.

We delayed leaving so many times out of fear. But we just had to go and get started. We departed the dock in close to gale-force winds. Once we were cleared of the dock it was a wonderful feeling of adventure. But that initial departure was gut-wrenching. I felt like throwing up. Letting go of the bowlines that first day we only ventured out about one-and-a-half miles from shore.

I had to get out of my comfort zone constantly during the trip. My stomach would be turning inside out, and I would feel like being sick—not because of the seas but because of the stress, yet I felt I couldn't let it show. All the courses we took and books we read didn't prepare us for everything that we were about to experience. We had never sailed in the open ocean and never sailed at night. There were many challenges that we had never done before.

There were times however my fear was almost paralyzing. The most harrowing time was when we had sailed on the Atlantic Ocean going from Florida to Nova Scotia and we were caught in a massive storm. Twenty-foot-high waves were too much. I felt like I was at the edge of the cliff, and it wouldn't take a lot to go over. The storm felt *overwhelming*. My kids and my wife looked to me for assurance that everything was going to be ok. I couldn't show them that I wasn't sure, that I was just as scared as they were. I couldn't even tell my wife how terrified I was. I had to show that we were under control and safe, otherwise there would be utter chaos.

In my mind, I broke the storm up into small sections and focused on what was in front of me. Forward was my focus for the next twenty-six hours as we made our way to Charleston, South Carolina, the closest main port. It felt good getting into the dock and knowing that we and our boat were safe. I was relieved and exhausted from both the physical and mental stress. At the time I often questioned myself and whether we were foolish to take those risks. Looking back at the two years at sea we had some incredible experiences, all because we got out of our comfort zone. We created a lifetime of lessons and memories for all of us.

LIFE TAKES A PERSONAL TURN

Although we weathered the storms of the high seas, our marriage didn't stand in longevity. As the children grew up, I realized that although we had a mutual love and respect for one another, we had grown apart and wanted different things. We both understood that life is too short and is not without risk and heartache. I decided that it would be best to divorce and for each of us to move forward with our lives than to remain together unhappy.

As with any divorce and family dynamic, it was not without its challenges. Breaking up is never an easy decision and with communication, we have been able to move forward in our own directions while remaining friends. The children, who were young adults already at that time, ventured on their own endeavors and career paths with support from each of us.

IDENTITY CRISIS

I always strived to be better and climbed the corporate ladder. I worked hard and was able to prove myself. Much of my identity was tied to my work. I had my mother's message etched in my mind: *you can do anything you want if you really want to*. And that I did.

After a very public firing in 2017, I was left struggling to figure out my identity. At the time I didn't know what to do. I felt lost and anxious. I was also very angry at how things unfolded. The CFO and CEO who signed off on the statements in question wanted to settle quickly. I could either fight it alone or join them and move on with my life. I reluctantly chose the latter. Exhausted and dejected I was broken.

My kids, and even my ex-wife, were incredibly supportive through this period and probably a little worried about me. I got up every day for a couple of weeks feeling like there was nowhere to go and nothing to do. I was scared. I was not prepared for this. At my age my career choices were limited. I didn't know what to do. It was an ugly situation, and I wasn't in control. The struggle to figure out what I was going to do next was pushing me down the rabbit hole emotionally. That empty feeling could have easily turned to depression.

The person I was dating was more concerned with the potential changes to her lifestyle than how I felt. She didn't provide me with support, and it really bothered me that our relationship was not what I thought it was. This was definitely a lesson. I needed to focus on my next steps and where my life was going to take me.

NEW CHALLENGES

Never was I more out of my comfort zone than starting up a business. Once I decided to start a gin distillery with my three kids, the feeling of emptiness was replaced by a high energy enthusiasm for this new challenge. This was my chance to work hard and have control and build something. I knew if it was the right business and I worked hard, it could be successful. I didn't have to answer to a board of directors or other management. My kids joined the business and off we went to conquer the gin world.

Starting the business was one of the most exciting and also stressful things I have ever done in my life. Even more stressful than dealing with actual pirates sailing in the Caribbean or public speaking before two thousand people or on television. A big part of that stress was the financial responsibility at a time in my life when most people are trying to slow it down and retire. Also, we had never made gin before. There were so many things we had never done before, but I took some comfort in doing these things with people I trusted: my kids.

Initially I never shared the financial fears that I had about the business with my kids. I felt that there was enough for them to worry about without adding to the stress levels. I couldn't let the business fail. Eventually I did keep them informed about the financial situation as I had just kept it all in and I needed an outlet. It was better being able to talk to them about it even if we didn't have a solution.

The pressure and stress of having to make every single decision weighed on me and my kids. There was no escaping it. It was also part of the fun in building your own business. I am very proud of what my kids and I created. There were problems and decisions to deal with every day which was both exhilarating and exhausting at the same time.

We won some awards for both our actual gin as well as our packaging and branding. Doing things the hard way had paid off. We were getting good coverage in social media and had developed a loyal following in a short period of time. We were a hit! I was having fun and felt really proud of not only what we had accomplished but how we got there.

We were open ten months when the COVID 19 pandemic changed all that making it a matter of survival. Within a week of the shutdown, we had laid off sixteen of our nineteen staff. I felt sick to my stomach every day throughout most of the pandemic. I made a list of equipment we could sell if we needed cash. I researched how to proceed through a bankruptcy. I was more scared than I think I had ever been in my career. I started to share that fear with the kids. We all bore the burden of stress through the pandemic.

I poured everything I had into this business. It sounded so romantic. Start a business with your kids and slowly ease into retirement as they take the reins and build the business. The reality was very different. One of the worst times to open a new business and yet we were getting an incredible response from customers. I couldn't let it fail and yet we were so close to failing. Part of me would have welcomed the business failing. It would have taken the pressure off and allowed me to relax.

It was a lot of long days and stomach wrenching worry. I kept telling my kids we just have to survive through the pandemic. At this stage of my life in my sixty's, it shouldn't be about survival. I didn't handle the stress very well. Dealing with a lot of it internally, I suffered two heart attacks in September of 2020. I'd had high blood pressure and cholesterol issues for many years. Bad genes, the doctors would tell me. Determined to deal with it naturally with diet and exercise, I even ran marathons when I turned fifty. It wasn't enough. This was a big wake-up call as to how fragile life can be; life became not just about survival for the business, but also for me personally. My parents had both passed away relatively young and I didn't want to add to the family statistics.

I had never had a scare like that and was lucky to be in the hospital when I had the second heart attack. The kids were great at taking some of the load off me and we talked a lot more openly about our struggles as a business and what I was feeling. We tried to restructure the business to get a better work-life balance. I tweaked what I thought was an already healthy lifestyle and agreed that it was time to take medication, and implement the recommended diet changes and exercise, into my daily regime. The thought of a life-threatening heart attack really scared me. I had too much in front of me to lose and look forward to. I enjoyed life far too much to let it slip away.

The stress will always be there, but I have learned how to manage it better. It doesn't matter how hard life knocks you down. You have to stand back up and keep moving forward. I have no regrets for ever getting out of my comfort zone, even when it didn't work out. It's how I've learned and grown in so many ways. It has also provided me with a wealth of experiences.

Yes, I will always be a factory worker's son. Although, when my father said it, he meant it as something limiting. I actually now look at it as a positive and steppingstone to everything. I learned so many things from both my parents, what to do and be and also the opposite. I realize that all of their hard work, and work ethic was the foundation that showed me that I could do it and more if you work hard. I am proud of my beginnings and journey. I also knew that I wanted more and never settled. Sometimes the lessons from your childhood are also what you don't want. I used the drive and determination combined with my parents' work ethic and commitment to sail to new adventures in life. Many days I miss sharing things with my parents. I constantly feel this need to prove myself to them, to know they would be proud. I look back at many of the things I have done and accomplished in amazement and think *wow,* while also looking forward with excitement.

The hardest thing to do is leaving your comfort zone.
But you have to let go of the life you're familiar with and
take the risk to live the life you dream about.

T. ARIGO

You deserve freedom. You owe it to
yourself. You are anything but selfish
whenever you decide to stand up
for yourself!

MYRIAM BEN SALEM

CARL RICHARDS

Carl Richards has spent more than twenty-five years behind the micro-
phone, entertaining and influencing audiences worldwide. He is a TEDx
Speaker and emcee, bestselling Author in The Soulology Chronicles:
Voices, host of the Speaking of Speaking Podcast and the founder and
CEO of Podcast Production Made Simple. Carl helps entrepreneurs
find their voice, launch world class podcasts and grow thriving and
profitable businesses. He lives with his spouse in Gananoque, Ontario,
Canada and enjoys boating in the 1000 Islands.

UNAPOLOGETICALLY ME

CARL RICHARDS

Obstacles don't have to stop you.
If you run into a wall,
don't turn around and give up.
Figure out how to climb it,
go through it, or work around it.

MICHAEL JORDAN

"Carl, stop and start again!"

I froze and stopped speaking. I paused, took a deep breath and started again. Sure enough, within three or four words, or a sentence, I started stammering and stuttering again. My parents repeated, *"Carl, stop, and start again!"*

For as long as I can remember, I stuttered. I don't remember when it started. When asking my mother, she seems to remember it starting right from the time I started speaking. I also don't know what caused it. In doing some research and some self and familial exploration, I did uncover a few things. Stuttering can be genetic. As far as familial, I do know my biological father Keith stuttered. From what my mother tells me, my 'dad's' stutter was pretty bad. According to my mother, he stuttered all his life. Not sure if there

71

was the kind of help for him there is today for kids who struggle with speech.

Someone told my parents not to correct me. Not say the word I was trying to say… but somehow they told me to stop and start again. This was always the scenario starting from when I was six years old. Eventually I stopped speaking altogether and only spoke when I absolutely had to. In school I would say to myself, *"please don't pick me."* I was terrified to be called on by the teacher to read out loud, even if it was a couple of sentences or a paragraph. This also brought on bullying and laughing by my peers.

Being a kid who stuttered was embarrassing. How did it make me feel? Humiliated. That I wasn't in control. I remember I used to get that feeling of terror throughout my entire body. My heart would race, my palms would sweat. Quite often I'd reach for something to grab and hold onto like a pen or tap my leg with my hand, or rub my hands together feverishly to get back in control of what I was saying. Once I got past 'the stutter' I would calm down… until the next stutter. I just wanted it to end.

GLIMPSE OF BOLD

Our family went to church every Sunday. At around eleven or twelve years old, I don't know what got into me that day, but I felt bold and confident to participate in the service by reading a passage. I put up my hand to volunteer and read from scripture. Standing at the front of the church on the pulpit, I opened the Good News Bible, the edition that we used in the Baptist church. A fairly easy read, even for a kid. However, once I started reading the passage, a wave of terror and fear permeated every cell of my body. Everyone in the congregation had their eyes on me.

As I began to read, I started stammering and stuttering. It seemed impossible for me to get through reading that passage. I was a wreck. Standing there at the front of the church, stuttering my way through, and getting hung up on words. It wasn't until the minister stood beside me, put his hand on my shoulder and started reading the words with me that I was able to finish reading that short scripture. I felt embarrassed, humiliated and realized I never wanted to do *that* again. *Ever.* I think a number of people in the church probably felt sorry for me and even felt my pain but didn't know what to say to me.

FINDING HELP

Stuttering is painful. In Sunday school,
I'd try to read my lessons, and the children
behind me were falling on the floor with laughter...
Speech is a very important aspect of being human.
A whisper doesn't cut it.

JAMES EARL JONES

It was Mrs. Pipe, my fifth grade teacher who helped my parents with a solution. She said there was help available for kids who stuttered. My folks did some follow-up with the school principal, who suggested speaking to our family doctor. The doctor did think that speech therapy was a definite possibility, and urged my parents to go through our local school board as the process would be quicker going direct. My parents discussed it with me and asked if I wanted to do it. I agreed. I had nothing to lose and everything to gain, if it worked. Truth be told I was afraid of what 'therapy' would entail.

Speech therapy wasn't individual. We were a group of boys all around the same age and would meet once a week with our speech therapist. I realized that my stutter wasn't as bad as some of the other boys in the group. The speech therapist gave us simple exercises and encouraged us to talk about our experiences that week. We would share things that we heard on the radio or other examples of stuttering that was commonplace. We didn't perceive it as stuttering... to us it was just normal speech. As we were sharing our experiences if we stuttered, he'd walk us through it, make us analyze the stutter and take control of our speaking, so to speak. Even if it meant making the stutter longer, the goal was to be in control.

While I was in speech therapy, there was one magical trick that I learned, which I now share with my clients. And that is, the only person in control of your speaking is you. There are other nuggets that I learned as well. For example, I learned that everybody stutters at some point in their life. A person who is labeled as a stutterer, what they are actually trying to do is block the stutter and make it sound perfect. And that's where the stammering comes from. I certainly didn't know that either.

TOWN TO TOWN UP AND DOWN THE DIAL

After two years of speech therapy, with my speech, I was, 'cured,' in a manner of speaking. Let's put it this way: I had some great tools that the speech therapist shared, and knew what to do if I felt a stutter coming on. The only logical thing to do at that point was decide to choose a career in performing arts. I chose radio broadcasting. Well, actually, before that, I thought the best thing would be is to become an actor. For every actor that makes it though, they're probably 20,000 that are working the fast food drive-thru asking *would you like fries with that?*'

So I thought there was a better chance of doing something I love through doing something else that I love. I always loved radio, because I thought it was theater of the mind. I listened to what was Top 40 Radio back in the 1980s and loved the idea of doing character voices. I actually did some impressions when I was fourteen. I figured that if I could do those with confidence, no doubt, I could perform on radio.

Pursuing that dream of being on the radio, I joined the high school radio club and read the announcements between first and second period. I was also instrumental in relaunching the Delta Radio Broadcast System (DRBS) which started playing music at lunch hour again in the cafeteria and in the hallways.

After graduating high school, I entered the radio broadcasting program in college where I worked tirelessly to hone the skills required to be a radio announcer. Graduating at the top of my class, I eventually landed that elusive first radio gig in a small town over 2000km (1300 miles) from home. One of the things I remember about being in a small town was how isolated I felt, and alone. It was similar to the way I felt when I stuttered; that nobody understood me, that nobody felt the same thing I did. It was also at that time that I was wrestling with my sexuality, and also felt silenced. I felt like I couldn't come out and say who I was and what I enjoyed. I couldn't say that I liked guys, because… well, that's just not something that you did in the late 1990s. Or if you did, and you worked in the public eye, there was always that risk of job loss or being ridiculed. I look back at it now and I wonder, what would have happened if I did actually come out then?

I spent four years continuing to perfect my craft. Eventually, I made my way back closer to home, to a larger market where I came face to face with the stutter again.

THE STUTTER REVISITED

I was hired to speak at an event in a local arena introducing a troupe of world renowned show horses called the Lipizzaner Stallions. I remember it vividly because most of the show was in the dark, with the lights off.

Before the introduction and warm welcome that I was about to give on behalf of the radio station, the lights in the whole arena were turned on and everyone's eyes were on me. At that very moment, I felt like I did back in church, reading that passage. I remember stammering a little bit, and stuttering. I tried to cover it up and make it seem like I was just caught up in the excitement of introducing the LLLLLLLLLLLLLipizzaner Stallions.

It's then that I realized that I needed to fix that. Stuttering wasn't going to beat me. I had this. On more than one occasion I had been invited to a Toastmasters meeting… and finally knew this time I had to say *"YES!"* So I went to Toastmasters and that's where I really gained my confidence back. I became a great Speaker, not just on radio but on stage as well, in front of live audiences. I competed in a speech contest and won, stepped into leadership roles within the organization and developed a love for public speaking. It was more than that though. Much deeper. I was developing a love and passion for helping other people with their pains that go around public speaking.

A lot of people are deathly terrified to speak in front of an audience. And I knew exactly what that felt like. So I made it my mission to help people not only with their presentation skills, but also to help them harness the *power* of their *own* voice. Still, however, I personally was feeling silenced.

SPEAKING OF BEING GAY

I continued to wrestle with my sexuality at that time too, as well as feeling unable to be honest and open and share from the heart. Because certainly there were things that I needed to keep quiet about. The broadcast industry is one that is hard enough to work in to begin with. It's a very cutthroat, very *'dog eat dog world.'* It's not unheard of for people to lose their jobs, *just because.* Reasons given could be maybe there are too many people working in that department. It's also not unheard of for people to lose their jobs because they're just not a *fit*. I always felt that if I came out of the closet and used my voice that I would be the next person on the chopping block. I didn't actually come out on the air and admit my sexuality publicly over the airwaves until I was forty-eight years old.

I think of all of those years living in fear. Fear of speaking, fear of being ridiculed, fear of being found out that I was gay. I think what I was really doing was gaining confidence to eventually come out fully. Not only admitting that I was a homosexual, but that I used to stutter. That made things very empowering to me.

People are quite often amazed when I tell them that I used to stutter when I was a kid. They would say in astonishment, *"Wow! But you speak so well."* I knew I was a good speaker and communicator. Not in a cocky way, but in a confident way. Speaking on the radio was *making* my confidence in one way, while I was *faking* my confidence in other ways, like using my voice to be fully powerful.

There was still a huge area of growth required for me. I lacked the confidence to say who I was. I didn't feel comfortable saying I was gay. I didn't even feel comfortable sharing fully with people my story about being a kid who stuttered. I used to just brush it off and give the *'Coles/Cliff Notes'* version of it. And it was actually a coach who shared with me that I should share that story in more detail and come from more of a feeling place. Because that's where the grit of the story really lies. It didn't lay in the fact that I was a kid who stuttered, it was the fact that I was terrified and I overcame that terror and fear. And even though I overcame one fear, there was still that fear of having my voice heard as a gay man.

Is it all related? Did somehow that all weave together? Some would say yes. And if I were to analyze it more closely, I would say that there are definitely some coincidences or parallels. But what I do know is this: in spite of feeling like I didn't have a voice until the age of fourteen and then even feeling that I didn't have a strong enough voice to fully admit to the world who I was, I eventually *did* take that first step. I faced that fear. I eventually did step forward and say, *"This is who I am."* I didn't do it in a dramatic way or as a means to draw attention to myself. I did it in a way that was subtle, yet assertive. I was no longer ashamed to call my husband just my spouse. I was okay referring to him by name, Jeff. *I was unapologetically me.*

EMBRACING ALL OF MYSELF

Today I stand up and speak with confidence without fear of judgment or repercussion. I don't give it a second thought when I start stuttering out of excitement and enthusiasm, on occasion, that still happens. I realize that the other part of having this feeling of confidence, is acceptance. Accepting myself for who I am and not looking for outside validation has been a huge transformation in my life. I spent most of my life searching for it and through my soul exploration, I now understand that acceptance *is* internal. That is the first step that has led me to future steps.

It has been through my personal experience, I now believe that, once we embrace and accept who we truly are and stop judging ourselves, we confidently flourish in our authenticity. Confidence and acceptance gives ourselves the permission to live in our power unapologetically and nothing can stand in our way.

Accept who you are; and revel in it.

MITCH ALBOM

You have to grow from the inside out. None can teach you; none can make you spiritual. There is no other teacher but your own soul.

SWAMI VIVEKANANDA

LISA RIZZO

Lisa Rizzo is a multi-published author and her words feed our souls. She is a Spiritual Medium as she was born with a gift to see things beyond our world. Her life is dedicated and spent fulfilling her purpose to be of service to many here on earth and beyond. Lisa's journey is forever continuing and evolving. She is supported by her loving family which includes her husband, children and grandchildren.

A PHOENIX HAS RISEN

LISA RIZZO

*Our wounds are often openings into
the best and most beautiful part of us.*

DAVID RICHO

Since the age of five, I have been able to connect with the spiritual world. I lived my life as a *spiritual being living a human existence* rather than a *human living a spiritual existence*. As a spiritual medium, I am used to seeing and hearing souls every day. My guides (angels) came to attend my calls when they were truly needed. I intrinsically knew that I could trust them to show me the way of things as they would happen in life or in the Universe.

Even though I was always with my family attending to their needs, I wasn't with them without spirit. Even my children would tell me, *"Mom, you need to stop giving yourself to others. We need you here in the present moment."* It wasn't uncommon in my home for anyone to ask me to take care of a headache or to ask, *"will I pass a test?"* This was our normal. We raised our children to be spiritual beings, kind and caring, and to be whoever they wanted to be in their lives as long as they are living as their true authentic selves.

A huge shift occurred, one that I found quite overwhelming. My world, as I knew it, turned inside out on physical Earth and beyond. Everything I had worked for and knew my entire life, changed, quite dramatically. For the first time in my life, I was *"alone."* I heard and felt nothing from the spirit world. It was devastating for me to hear and feel nothing but silence. It felt daunting and empty not having them with me at all times.

I realize that this had to happen as I needed to learn to trust my own gut feelings. In the upcoming, new awakening, I needed to see with my own eyes and feel everything. I would go through many things without expecting guidance outside of myself. My spirit guides told me years ago that there was something coming. They said that we all need to be prepared to make many changes in our spirit, minds, and bodies to be able to serve our great purpose in this life as we have lost our way. Everything will become clear and we will no longer walk around with blinders. There will be a choice for those people who are willing to connect spiritually and to intuitively raise the vibration of humanity in a global way. Many will not make the transition to a new conscious mindset as it will be too overwhelming for them, and for many souls walking with blinders on will be easier and more comfortable. We are all energy and connected to one another. It is through that connectivity that we can raise our collective vibrations for the greater good and manifest our destiny.

Imagine if everything you thought you *knew* was to disentangle and reveal itself. I was on a journey with the Universe and the spirit world. The future of humanity and how everything I ever understood about my own spirituality was going to completely unravel. Many personal things—both good and bad—took place for me and my family; I'm blessed to have been able to help. But I didn't realize that in order to make sense of it all, I was drowning in my own consumption of past and present aggressions.

THE SOUND OF SILENCE

In the beginning of my *shutdown* (the time during which I had no spiritual connections), I started to feel everything and everyone. I knew in my forties that I was given *"the understanding"* by my guides, that I had the ability to walk between both the light and the darkness. Which side will you allow to flourish? That was the question. I was being tested by both the darkness and the light.

This meant that I couldn't close the worlds between the living or the deceased and the frequencies were extremely loud. I would suffer from migraines for days. The pressure felt too much to bear, but I had to push through as I always have. As I continued to serve my purpose as a spiritual medium, I thought to myself, *Dear Guides: I am ready for my next calling.*

Then the chaos started. My family would wake up from nightmares or hear or feel a presence in the house. My granddaughter would wake up in the middle of the night screaming. My family couldn't understand why I wasn't able to send these spirits away or how they were even entering our home. I was confused and angry that I was unable to keep my family safe from the spirit world. I would cry at night and force myself to stay awake to be present if a spirit came through, good or bad.

This was only the beginning of my world turning upside down. Within a year, our family was being broken apart, everyone was overwhelmed with fear and stress of the unknowns. Prior to this, we took everything day by day and we loved being together. I realized this was the workings of the darkness; it was trying to push me to the edge. My family means everything to me so I worked harder on my meditations and my lightwork with my ancestors and Mother Earth. I knew I was being broken and consumed. Bit by bit I was crumbling to ash. I still didn't know why but I had faith in my heart and soul that I could overcome this.

THE PORTAL

The next stage to this transformation was excruciating pain throughout my body. I saw many doctors and had what seemed like endless medical tests, and they all came back normal. This began back in 2004, and I tried to excuse it as *"just aging"* although I knew in my soul it had nothing to do to with age. But how do I tell a doctor, *"Excuse me, I'm being tested by the darkness and it needs me to fail in life or a test?"* Well, of course, I couldn't. I started to live in an unfamiliar world to me, the *human living a spiritual existence*. I was eventually diagnosed with fibromyalgia.

From the physical pain, my torment expanded to the unconscious. I started to have recurring dreams in which I would see myself lying on the ground with *"my"* wings stuck in quicksand. I didn't understand why I was dreaming this repeatedly. I felt in my soul that my guides were trying to give me hints or signs, but I wasn't sure what the messages meant. At that point, my spirit guides were still absent and not communicating as they used to.

One day I woke up and had this inspiration to go within myself to see if there are any uncleared, unopened *"doors"* of self-awareness in my soul. What I discovered was that there were many things buried deep in my unconscious mind that I thought I had resolved years before. I knew if I was going to open these doors or portals, I had to be prepared for anything. As I have told many others, I was given the choice to serve all in light and in darkness, here and beyond. It was now time to make that choice and take my own journey. The Creator was doing this for a bigger purpose. I believed that and trusted it. This was a huge shift for me to take. Being a vessel and serving others has always been me. Serving others. This was really the first time that I had devoted *all* of my energies solely to myself. I was going deep within my own psyche.

The pain in my body got worse and I was physically breaking down even more; the darkness was taking over my spirit. I was crumbling physically and emotionally. This is what the darkness wanted from me. It wanted me to give up on myself, humanity, and the spiritual world. This went on for years. I struggled to fight my fears and to keep my faith. I had to believe and trust that one day, this was all going to make sense.

GETTING MY WINGS

Through soul searching, I once again called out to my guides to ask if I'm ready to take on my next journey with the spiritual world. I have been given many tasks in my lifetime and each one giving me more purpose to serve our Creator. I'm sharing what my guides have been showing me for years now. I have been very quiet listening to the world, connecting with thousands of spirit walkers by pure energy. They have been going through the same tasks as I have, and in the same order.

My guides finally reconnected with me, which brought tears to my eyes. I could feel their warmth and love which, once again, filled my soul. I knew I had done the work I needed to do for myself and opened all the portals within to set myself free from unwanted fears that I didn't even know were deep inside my soul. My wings were no longer in the quicksand as foretold in my recurring dream. Now I understood the signs that were sent to me. I had to focus on myself to move forward to the next level in my metamorphosis and purpose.

I could see in my guides' eyes the concern. I asked them, *"Where have you been?"* I've been blessed with the same spirit guides my whole life, which doesn't happen very often. I knew their presence; they didn't have time to explain, so I just listened and absorbed. They asked me to stop any readings or group sessions, not to use my energy or my gift to serve humanity or the spirit world at that very moment.

I thought I had done everything they asked of me. I did shut down my work connecting people with the spirits years ago. I was so confused. I realized at that moment, that I would often open up to people and souls that were just passing through, people and souls who wanted answers and yet they had not even asked me. I was to hold on to my energy and keep the realm between spirit and people closed. Something was coming and I needed to be prepared for as thousands of us (spiritual mediums) received the same message. I accepted and did what I was asked. Even though my vessel (body) was in pain and weak, I was ready. I still had a fight within my soul to do whatever I was going to be asked.

My guides told me it was time to see everything that the Universe wanted me to see with my third eye. I was completely unprepared to see all that the spirits showed me was headed our way, for both humanity and the spirit world. I was confused at first. The first thing that my guides shared with me was shocking. I wasn't ready to hear what I was going to hear.

I was told I was one of Archangel Michael's descendants. There are millions of us around the world. It felt crazy to hear that and crazier to come to terms with it. I cried in disbelief for days. How was I going to tell my family? I never keep them out of my visions with my spirit guides. They have seen and gone through all my predictions and are witness to my truths. Well did I tell them? Yes, I did, and it made so much sense after looking at what I had gone through.

My guides shared with me that I was among many *fallen angels* coming into the new world, and that the "The Awakening" I had been talking about for years would soon be upon us. My guides explained to me that they needed to leave me, to prepare me for what's ahead, so I could help others. I had to experience the physical world, the pain, despair, and confusion. I had to clear all that was not serving me so I could emerge as the phoenix. This rise took years, starting in my forties. I was at the time of these messages, fifty-two.

HUMANITY

It has been shown to me personally and to the millions of us in our community that we, the fallen angels, have come back to walk amongst the living to help prepare humanity for their choices in this life. The choices are clear: To either keep being conditioned by our ego and greed *or* awaken to see our Creator's living things are dying. My job is to connect with all fallen angels in energy within this world, as well as the fallen angels that are beyond. I am to protect the souls in the realm between both worlds, as well as the ones trying to descend to the physical world, so they can be reborn or return to the realm.

I can tell you; many souls do not want to return to this world. It weighs too heavy on their souls that the darkness is in the lead at this moment. The darkness has told me that it is the choice of our *"free will."* We have the free will to choose what to feed: either the *"The Dark or The Light"* of humanity as a whole. We are at war, and we don't even understand how. I see what is coming for our humanity and spirit, mind, and body, as people in power serve the darkness. There is work to be done and there isn't any more time to turn our heads the other way. I know now that I was sent here to prepare my children and grandchildren as much as possible before I return to the realm myself. I walk without organized religion but I have faith in humanity, the Universe, and the Creator who resides in all of us. I have seen these days coming and so have many spirit walkers.

The spirit world has told me that people will have to go through many losses and over many things. Humanity as a whole is going to have to make a choice: each of us must either use our *"free will"* or live like a prisoner of war, meaning, do what you are told and comply, or get back to the basics in the past and present. *"Free will"* was a gift given to all of us. We have a responsibility to this world and our descendants. The *"Darkness and the Light"* have been in many wars. If we don't start to help the awakening, we will fail ourselves and our Creator.

Can you imagine how I am feeling? I'm trying to live a normal life knowing what is coming our way. Look what has already taken place around the world. For me to be in meditation every day means that I'm always at *work* and I'm very tired. The one question I asked my guides was *"how am I going to share this with my fifth sense to people without them being overwhelmed or stressed with anxiety?"* They guides said, *"Lisa, so many are already suffering from all these things. They are the Creator's souls and they have the Divine's hopes within them. They have just lost their way."*

My mouth dropped: it was so true. It started to make so much sense to me. I've been suffering from fibromyalgia for years. Some days I couldn't even function as it took over my vessel (body). The darkness wanted me weaker, so it would make it easier to take over my body.

CHAOS TO CLARITY

My empowerment, courage, and strength come from my faith and knowing that I will forever continue to serve, living in my light and goodness for a greater purpose. I am called to help people to reach their highest selves without fear and judgment. My alignment lies with those who are mentally and spiritually moving forward in their enlightenment journey. I have a *"knowing"* that my destination is to guide the newly gifted, the ones who have tapped into their spiritual and intuitive mindsets.

Through my experience, I view myself as a phoenix rising from the ashes. I have learned that we all have the ability to discover our own soul's purpose. "The Awakening" and finding our soul's purpose happens when we choose to seek knowledge and truth. It is all about self-awareness and the perception of your own reality. This reality may cause confusion and chaos at the beginning of awakening. It is a process, and it can be a messy one. The journey to reaching one's personal destination, is accomplished through seeking knowledge and truth *beyond* the narrative presented by the masses. The process of awakening is on a continuum and dynamic in nature. That *"inner knowing"* is a gut feeling which is a sign to guide us to our own path of light while recognizing the darkness around us. This knowing allows us to use our free will to consciously choose goodness over darkness.

I have discovered my own version of clarity and have seen the transformation of others. I know that we all have that phoenix within us. We rise and fall throughout our lives. Every time we fall, we open wounds that require *"the work"* so you can move forward and heal. It is with *that* rise, we gain clarity and come back even more powerful than were before.

And when all that was left was ashes, she would again clothe herself in flame. Rising from the dust of her past to rekindle the spark of her future. She was a Phoenix, her own salvation; rebirthed, renewed, resurrected.

LARHONDA TORESON

No matter how you define success,

you will need to be resilient,

empowered, authentic, and

limber to get there.

JOANIE CONNELL

STEPHANIE ROBINSON

Stephanie Robinson is a published author, a leader in healthcare innovation and team builder. She holds a Masters Degree in clinical psychology and is the Chief Operating Officer of Open Mind Health. Stephanie is a skilled psychotherapist/executive coach and a sought-after consultant for mental health systems. As a true visionary, Stephanie is a results-driven, compassionate and insightful transformational force of growth and well-being for individuals, teams and organizations.

TOO MUCH MUCHNESS

STEPHANIE ROBINSON

You will always be too much of something for someone;
too big, too loud, too soft, too edgy.
If you round out your edges, you lose your edge.

DANIELLE LAPORTE

People would say I had *"grit and tenacity"* and others would comment that I was *"too much."* The latter two words stung and made me feel exposed. I had always longed to appear polished but could never master it. I felt like I was pulling my sleeves down over my hands, but nothing could hide the dirt under my fingernails from clawing my way through life. I would watch beautiful women and feel nothing in common with them. I envied these women; they looked like perfect Disney princesses, untarnished. I impulsively overcompensated, by smiling too hard and talking too loudly. I did everything I could to prove that I was smart, capable, and productive—driven by the fear of never being enough. The words *"too much"* and the dismissals plucked on that sensitive nerve—that nerve that throbbed whenever my fear of being worthless, annoying, and a burden kicked in.

Watching The Little Mermaid with my daughter; she pointed to the TV: *"Look Mommy,"* she said. *"Ariel combs her hair with a fork, isn't that funny?"* It hit me hard because I combed my hair with a fork when I was my daughter's age. In fact, I had felt lucky and even a little clever to have imagined how useful a fork would be. I mean the last thing I wanted to hear was my second-grade teacher tell me *again, "You look like you are raised by wolves."* We didn't have a brush in the house, and my father admittedly had *no* idea what to do with me. I reflect back now and realize, I was like a Disney princess, a real-life combination of so many of them. I was a motherless, abandoned, and neglected child.

Acknowledging these descriptors forced me to face the deep truth of an emptiness in the pit of my stomach that overshadowed almost every moment in my life. I didn't feel a sense of belonging anywhere or to anyone. There was a freedom in that to some extent, I told myself. I took pride in being a born leader. I was a unique character and I felt empowered in being responsible for others. But underneath that surface, I feared closeness as much as I feared abandonment. I over empathized with anyone in emotional or psychological pain because it amplified my own, yet was drawn to them, having a deep need to relieve their suffering. But I learned that taking on someone else's pain also denied them the dignity in the lessons they needed to learn.

Throughout my life I tried to ease the feeling of not belonging by trying to camouflage myself to fit in. However, avoiding attention and flying under the radar to be invisible was always short-lived. I would start by pretending to want to fit in but would soon reject the mainstream, or I would intentionally stand out. I *am a lot* of woman in the core of my being—in my physical being, in my emotional intensity, and spiritually. I just vibrate at a different frequency and cannot be tamed. Thus, I've often felt clumsy, annoying and like I was a nuisance.

Anxiety fueled by fear of worthlessness, emptiness, and loneliness has both overshadowed and propelled me much of my life. As a little girl, I would steal my father's pillows, wrap them in blankets, and pile them beside me to pretend it was my mother lying next to me, only to freak myself out in the middle of the night thinking my pretend person was a real dead body. To this day, I still hate to sleep alone. I also resisted going to bed and would lay on the floor looking out the crack at the bottom of the door, just to make sure I wasn't alone.

Dad would say *"go play in the traffic"* when I would seek his attention. My ex-husband would pinch me or punish me for laughing too loud or smiling too much. Bosses would tell colleagues to think out of the box, *"But not you, Stephanie. You need to stay inside the box with your unrealistic aspirations."*

LITTLE WOMAN

One night, when I was six, I realized my father had gone to sleep at his girlfriend's house leaving my younger brother and I all alone. I sat outside my brother's door in case he woke up. I didn't want him to be afraid. Worrying about him, allowed me to put my own feelings aside. I felt very grown up: fierce, independent, and purposeful.

I thought of my mother, who two years earlier—when I was four years old—had been dragged to the psychiatric ward and diagnosed with schizophrenia. My brother, when in his teens was also diagnosed with schizophrenia; he had never been *quite right.* I felt abandoned by her. I thought of my father's loneliness. Both of his parents had passed and he lost his wife within a handful of years of each other. He resented that he became a single parent because of my mother's hospitalization and wasn't prepared for that role.

I didn't want to burden him or anyone else. I decided that moment, *I will not grow up to be a single parent, and I don't think kids should be left home alone.* I felt a kind of clarity in my decisiveness and a strength to set an intention for a different path for my life. Yes, I was six years old. That one decision changed the course of my life. Feeling in control—empowered—was, and has been, the only emotion that trumped the feeling of worthlessness.

In the years following, I found myself at many crossroads where being a determined, decisive, action-taker propelled me. Each time I remember having this feeling of being in *"the zone."* In that zone, I could feel my mind, body, and spirit in perfect alignment. I *knew* what I needed to do, even when others thought my decisions were misguided. And sometimes, they were. Few of those early roads were easy, leading many people to ask why I insisted on choosing the hardest roads.

PATH OF MOST RESISTANCE

Sometimes the right path
is not the easiest one.

GRANDMOTHER WILLOW
POCAHONTAS

The need to be so independent—being unwilling to trust grown-ups from so early on—took its toll on me. I wanted to get out. At the age of ten, not only did I look older than I was, but I also felt older than I do today. That was the first time I ran away from home. A couple years later, when I was twelve, my dad said, *"If you want out of this house so bad go ahead and get pregnant, you will see."* I took notice. That threat, I am sure, was meant to dissuade me, but it actually felt like a reasonable exit plan. I considered it among the principle steps I would need to take to gain my freedom.

I fantasized about creating a peaceful space for myself and having a baby to pour all my love into. I longed for that unconditional love and acceptance. I was a virgin at twelve but now I had a plan. I started to look for apartments and furniture in the newspaper Buy and Sell section, which led me to running away again: this time I managed to stay away for three months. I lied about my age and got a job as a live-in nanny. That situation went to shit when the mother of the two-year-old I was taking care of ran away to *"find herself."* I asked a neighbor to take the child and me in when we ran out of food.

The police found me and placed me in a youth detention home. There where locks on the doors and mysterious punishments for kids that went AWOL. I actually had no desire to leave there; I felt safe and free to be myself. I took charge, managed and mobilized all of the other kids, organizing games to keep them interested in their chores. The staff really appreciated it and I felt purposeful and important.

After a quick stint in foster care, I was returned to my father's home, but being back *"home"* was short-lived. Following through with my plan to escape, I was pregnant by the age of fourteen. Obviously, my father was not happy and had his girlfriend set up an appointment for an abortion. As he warned me years before, I was not allowed to stay at his house if I kept the baby. The doctor told me that if I didn't want the abortion, not to come to the next appointment. I *knew* the only answer was to run away on the night before the appointment. I found a couple that let me stay with them but the apartment was crawling with cockroaches. That was no place for a baby, so I called child protection services. I successfully negotiated with them: I would turn myself in *if* they took me to the group home for unwed mothers I had researched.

I spent the next nine months reading every parenting book I could find. Adoption advocates visited me frequently. I accepted their attention but nothing they would say would dissuade me. Why would a mother *give up* their child? It was a question I asked my own mother when my daughter was four (the age I was when she gave me up). I finally understood that she wasn't able to care for me, given her schizophrenia.

Besides, I wasn't alone anymore—I was Michelle's mother. As she looked up at me when I cradled her, I promised her I would never leave her alone. I promised myself I could have my own adolescence when she grew up, like when she was fourteen (in some perverse way that became the age of adulthood to me). Until then, I would go to school, work hard, and be the kind of woman that would make her proud. As I look at my own parenting style, I realize that I vacillated between under compensating to build independence in her and overcompensating by fiercely protecting for fear of losing her.

By the age of nineteen, I had given birth to my second child. *No one would ever know my struggle*, I thought. I hit all the milestones, got married at twenty-four, bought my first house at twenty-five, and graduated university with my age cohorts, all while often trekking my two kids to school with me. I was determined. I clawed my way through, and later escaped what became an abusive, tumultuous marriage.

While trying to secure myself and my kids, my son was diagnosed with insulin dependent diabetes and refused to take his insulin while I was at work. The doctor gave me an ultimatum: *"Quit your job and stay with him or put him in foster care."* An inconceivable dilemma, with a single income, mortgage, and no child support, how would I manage? That trusted, empowered, and decisive feeling kicked in. I *knew* what to do. I became a specialized foster parent for kids with diabetes, and at the same time, I pursued my graduate degree in clinical psychology. Caring for three teenagers, two with complex medical needs, plus a night job at an addiction treatment center, I carried the weight of the world on my shoulders. But I had a sense of purpose and belonging, unconditional love, as well as an anxiety disorder.

CINDERELLA

At thirty-three it donned on me that I was a grownup. It's that painful reality of life when it sinks in that *yes* you are *free* to do as you like, but, Cinderella, you have to get up for work in the morning, so clean the *"castle"* and get your ass to bed. I realized I built my own *"do right"* fortress. The path had been a long and difficult one. I was fearful now of stepping too far outside the lines. I did not want to make any more mistakes.

I looked at life and leadership differently. I humbly came to accept that maybe I didn't know better than *them*. I realized that parents were just people. Even though I read all the books, had the very best of intentions, and attempted to be *"perfect,"* I made mistakes as a parent, but I knew I couldn't run away from home anymore when things got tough. I embraced the saying *"No matter where you go, there you are."* The thought of running was futile as no one was coming to take care of these kids and I made them a promise: I would always be there for them.

When things got tough, people would ask, *"How do you do it?"* I would answer, *"I have no choice."* Several times I was corrected: *"Yes you do have choices, Stephanie; you just keep making the right ones."* I took pride in my radical optimism, hard work, selflessness, and fierce independence. I believed that I was a *freedom fighter*; it was my purpose. However, I did get weary with my motivation, as it was fueled mainly by fear of emptiness settling in and of being abandoned.

My hair was a mess, my clothes needed to be sewn. The situation screamed that I needed to be *"saved."* But how if I could never *really* allow anyone get too close to me. I sabotaged my own happiness. *"I can do it all by myself, so love me at your own risk,"*

I would dare them, all while secretly wishing for *someone, anyone* to carry a burden for me.

One of my coping strategies was that I needed to believe in possibilities and to see the world as it *ought* to be, not necessarily as it *was*. I needed magic to counterbalance the struggles as I held on and hoped for better. I also realized along the way how much other people needed to borrow my radical optimism when they started to get disillusioned or had faced too much ugly shit. People need to believe everything is possible. Many times, that was the only thing I held onto that saved me from the depths of fear, or worse: apathy and despair. I finally understood that it all came down to me. I didn't *need* magic. I needed to believe in myself.

> *You control your destiny,*
> *you don't need magic to do it.*
>
> MERIDA, BRAVE

YOU FANCY, HUH?

I was certainly more edgy than the fancy, polished professionals I worked with. I was educated too, but by *both* books and the streets. It occurred to me that I could integrate my grittiness—my muchness, this love I had for the over-the-top glitter and glam. I mean, *why choose?* That *is* me being my authentic self, after-all. I was confident in myself, my abilities, and my achievements; yet, I did have a pre-conceived belief that I still wasn't as worthy as the *"beautiful, educated, and bougee"* people. I mean, *"Look at them—they do not have to struggle like I did,"* or so I thought.

Two key people helped me see this differently, one being my real-life Fairy Godmother a.k.a. my stepmother. She mediated for my father and I to reconcile our differences and helped both him and I to see the sparkly parts of me. She was a practical woman—a strict German school principal—but she loved to indulge me with tons of attention and sparkly gifts. She encouraged me to apply for a new job close to where she lived so we could be *"the ladies who lunch."*

That move would change the trajectory of my life. I met the yang to my yin—the second key person who really saw me, Dr. Craig Beach. It wasn't like one of those magical meetings where you just know you will be forever friends. Not at all in fact. But, in a job interview, he saw something in me that no one else at the table did. Dr. Beach was the psychiatrist for this new innovative, collaborative, multidisciplinary team I was hired to lead. Craig told me after I started that he had demanded they hire me because I had *"huge balls."* I thought, *"Oh my God! Are they showing again?"*

While although this was my dream job, one that allowed me to have real purpose by treating the most seriously mentally ill people, Craig challenged the fuck out of me. I had to navigate between his unreasonably high expectations for clinical care, the capabilities of the staff tasked with executing the plans, and the underfunded, siloed, toxic and broken mental health system which would need to evolve and make way if this model was to have a fighting chance. But evolve and make way had been my only way of moving this far, and true to form, once again I took the hard road.

I was given the opportunity to grow my own team. I was able to be my most authentic self in all of my eclectic and sometimes bossy muchness. Craig was brilliant—an ivy-league educated psychiatrist who was always on top of the most cutting-edge research for improving care. To top it off, he looked like a daytime soap opera star: fancy and polished. Yet, what I admired most was his deep empathy and his ability to push the boundaries and challenge people to get the best *for* and *from* them.

One evening, feeling rather fancy, drinking "Châteauneuf-du-Pape" (The Dirty Bottle), and watching the sunset, I realized just how comfortable I felt to be myself around him, partly because I was sure I couldn't fake a thing. I believed he could read my mind, that he could see through me. He was a psychiatrist after all! *Does he know I've spent most of my life waiting for schizophrenia to ravage and warp my mind like it did my mother and brother?* I wondered. Craig leaned over to me and it became clear he felt he could also be himself around me. He told me of his own limiting beliefs. At first I thought he was mocking me, until he told me his story.

We joked about the bottle of wine before us. The Dirty Bottle was a symbol of each of us. A perfectly balanced, full-bodied red wine from the South of France. The bottle is designed to be warped and look dirty. The back story for the brand was its produce had been through a fire that warped the bottle but could not affect the value and personality of the wine, and in fact, only made it more beautiful. Craig and I now laugh and say, *"If you have nothing nice to say, smile and say it in French."*

Sometimes we only see how people are different from us.
But if you look hard enough, you can see how much we're all alike.

JASMINE, ALADDIN

BELLE OF THE BALL

Craig was in a weird way my Prince Charming, my best friend, and a gay dude, but we have had many wonderful adventures together. A pivotal adventure occurred while we were on a gay cruise through the Mediterranean. People thought it strange I was going and cautioned me out of concern that I wouldn't fit in, or worse, that I'd be rejected as an imposter when the gay men on the cruise realized I was straight.

Well, they couldn't have been more wrong. As a matter of fact, I was the most popular girl on the ship and all our new fancy, accomplished, and fun friends took such good care of me, I felt like a queen. I finally felt it all come together; these are my people. I felt that I was validated and appreciated for being my authentically gritty self, laughing too loud, smiling too big, and loving too much. It was a powerful experience, and I have learned and given myself permission to embrace all of myself ever since.

On one warm August evening at an all-white party on the cruise, standing at the top of the spiral staircase, dressed in a gown with big silver and crystal costume jewelry, I gazed at the crowd below and felt it all came together. A talented New York City artist played the grand piano and people were dancing. Craig and I were drinking Martinis from a bar made of ice.

As I surveyed the scene, it hit me: I felt like Cinderella and the belle of the ball. I giggled: this is sure not a traditional fairy tale. My feet were firmly planted and the only thing sweeping me off my feet or posing as my white knight was the Tesla Model 3 I bought myself for my birthday. It was a trip of a lifetime and better than a fairy tale as it was real and not fleeting. *This* Cinderella paid for her own ticket and her own shoes when we stopped to shop in Sicily.

It dawned on me, I had even surpassed and outgrown Cinderella. I smiled to myself, straightened my crown, and acknowledged *"I am a matriarch and I am a queen."* This is what it was all for.

Imperfection is beauty, madness is genius and it's
better to be absolutely ridiculous than absolutely boring.

MARILYN MONROE

You were put on this earth to achieve
your greatest self, to live out your
purpose, and to do it courageously.

STEVE MARABOLI

ROE SARITA

Roe has spent most of her professional life in the hospitality industry in New York City, which led to her owning a restaurant. However, she always dreamed of becoming a storyteller. After closing the restaurant due to the pandemic, Roe returned to the art of writing and has realized her dream as a published author. Grateful for the reset to heal and find her voice, she is reconnecting with her childhood, where she spent her days immersed in the abundant nature of a small village in Guyana.

THE RESCUE

ROE SARITA

It takes a hell of a lot of courage to walk into your own story, but to be the hero of your own life you have to rescue yourself.

SHANNON L. ALDER

I've often described my childhood as idyllic when in fact I now understand that it was the beginning of my trauma. I grew up in a small coastal village in Guyana. The ocean was close enough to our house that I fell asleep to the sound of waves every night. I cling dearly to those memories of home and the ocean which was our backyard. Life was so simple then. The vastness of that ocean. I was in awe of her. How *she* could get volatile and wreck ships, yet she was the most nourishing loving parent to me; she made me feel small yet infinite at the same time. I felt my breath in the rhythm of her waves and often thought of her as existing within me, within my heart, even when I was far away.

I was a quiet child. I can't exactly explain what it was other than feelings of fear and numbness. I was scared to speak. My aunt who raised me said that I shook my head or nodded when anyone asked me a question. My purpose in life, I was told, was to become a good cook, so that I could be a good wife to someone one day. That was culturally the way of life and what was expected of me. I thrived in the unspoken language of the kitchen, in the fluid movements around the stove. There is still so much for me to unpack about my challenge with language and fear of speech.

I was raised in a poor village of strong women, who knew *"their place."* They kept chickens, cooked three times a day, and worked on the rice paddies, some with a toddler or two tied to their backs. When they weren't cooking, they were prepping for the next day: soaking beans, sifting rice, putting okra out in the sun to dry. Despite their strength, commitment, and hard labor, many women struggled due to their husband's constant violent wrath, often brought on by alcohol abuse. They sat on their verandas after dinner, an intermission from their beatings. I often thought about the women who were not sitting outside at sunset and wondered if they were okay, concerned they couldn't catch a break.

I spent most of my childhood on the veranda with my aunt who was one of these strong women. One day, she fought back and it worked. My uncle stopped drinking after she threw a glass bottle filled with her sewing needles at him. Although my uncle stopped bullying her, she did not stop bullying my brother and me.

My aunt raised me and my brother because our parents were in New York working, like so many other immigrant families, to live the *"American Dream."* Once they were stable, they would send for me and my brother. My parents sent money to my aunt every month, yet she took *every* opportunity she had to remind my brother and myself that we were taking up space at her dinner table, that our parents abandoned us, that we were not loved, not by anyone. We were bound to her for shelter. She often reminded us to do our chores and earn our space. Despite her contempt for us, I loved her.

There weren't many books for children my age in the village, but my aunt had a locked bookcase with a few literary hardcovers reserved only for her child, who was not allowed to do chores. I remember asking to read one of her books and was given the key *once* to select one book for an hour. That was the first and last time. So, when my aunt included me in her magical world of cooking, it was the only time I felt any sense of belonging. I was her little helper, proud to be included, and always eager and ready to cook with her after school and on the weekends. I unconsciously connected food with love.

Once the visas arrived for my aunt and her family to move to the United States, my aunt called our parents to tell them she was selling the animals, getting rid of furniture, and all of the things in the home. She wasn't going to stick around to make arrangements for me and my brother. Hearing that was literally like a knife through my heart, and I fell to the floor. I was twelve years old. My father left for New York when I was two, my mother when I was four. My brother and I didn't know our parents. All we knew was our life in the village with my aunt and her family. I didn't realize that all I endured would build my inner strength.

Mom and Dad did come to our rescue after our aunt left us. I had lived my life in that village without these two people who were supposed to be my parents. Their title as parents didn't really mean much to me during that year when they returned to us in Guyana.

THE AMERICAN DREAM

I turned thirteen the month we moved from Guyana to a basement apartment in Queens, a borough in New York City. My brother was sixteen. Being there, so far from my quiet village, was a true culture shock. Not only was it rough living with these strangers called *"parents"* but we lived in a very tough area of the city. I went to school and made it through junior high whereas my brother dropped out of high school six months after we arrived. Instead of the ocean and listening to the waves in my backyard, I heard the train. I drifted in and out to the clattering noise, the New York noise.

Not at all the dream life I had been told about and envisioned. I discovered that my dad was a violent and horrible drunk, my mom his enabler. I witnessed violent and tumultuous episodes. My brother was not around much as he made friends and followed a path based on his own thirst for life, so I was with them, basically alone.

I tried to protect my mother whenever I could. As no thirteen-year-old should, I fought my father off my mother on many occasions. I hid the knives and all the sharp objects during his worst fits, grabbed at him when he squeezed my mother's neck between the door, pushed him away when she fell to the ground after he threw the coffee table on her. My father's family was disappointed with *me* for the 911 calls that led to him being arrested on several occasions. My aunts, including the one who raised me, were convinced I lied about his behavior and that I was nothing but a lost, disrespectful teenager who *dared* to refer to her father as an alcoholic. They gasped when I pleaded with them to convince him to get help. He didn't go for help and the tirades didn't stop. I felt suffocated and did whatever I could to not be home. I just wanted to get out.

To cope, I buried myself in extracurricular activities after school for years. I enrolled in just about everything I saw on the bulletin board. I also volunteered at a nearby nursing home and at the local YMCA. During my second year at a community college near home, I realized I had no direction and no idea of what I wanted to study. I was turning twenty and at home on a Friday night watching television. I saw something on TV that made me realize I was living only a bridge and tunnel away from one of the greatest cities in the world. I decided it was time to get to know the real New York City. So later that week I set out to find a waitressing job in NYC. After a few months I was earning enough money to support myself. It was time to start on my own adventures.

I moved out of my parents' house to a Brooklyn apartment with my first roommate, a customer I became friends with. She was like the sister I never knew I needed. There was so much to learn about my body, about hygiene, about how to dress for the seasons and why I needed to own winter boots, rain boots, spring shoes, and summer sandals. The first few years working in NYC was a sensory overload. Even taking an elevator for the first time was intimidating. It took me some time to tell the difference between an apartment building and a hotel and the car rides were the worst. Growing up in a village, we had no reason to own a car. We often rode on the back of someone else's donkey cart or once in a while, we would ride the back of someone's truck standing, holding onto the rails, with the wind beating on our faces. The sounds of the city's constant bustling were not soothing or grounding like the crashing of the ocean's waves that I carried in my soul. How I missed her.

My mother had expected that I would remain in college, get an amazing job, and remain at home until I got married, as was the norm in our culture. As the first in our immediate family to make it past high school, I adjusted to my newfound freedom, knowing how important college was to my family; however, I encountered a problem. Supporting myself and going to college was impossible. I dropped out and worked my way to bartending from waitressing and stayed there for many years. I was free from my parents but trapped in a lifestyle of working to pay the rent, literally one dollar at a time. My survival depended on how much someone tipped me but freedom from my family was incredibly rewarding. It was a new chapter, I was in servitude and survival mode, but finding joy in serving others.

FOOD FOR THOUGHT

I lived a very quiet life and didn't date much. When I met my husband at age twenty-seven, I'd had only one boyfriend before. He was the typical New York City chef: a high-strung, bourbon drinking, chain smoker, with a work hard, ready-to-punch-some-one attitude. To me, he was a needle in a haystack, a loner, a homebody, just like myself. That was all we had in common. We were introverted extroverts who enjoyed the quiet respite of home life after work, a rare thing to find in the restaurant industry. He liked to drink at home instead of going out to a bar after work and I liked him precisely for that reason.

After almost a decade of bartending, I was burnt out, jaded even, and annoyed at people. The magic of the city began to fade. I had been thinking of transitioning out of hospitality so after only six months of dating, when I was in all honesty, giddy with joy, we talked about marriage. I wanted something to change in my life and I just went along with it. I figured this was it. I said yes just as I was discovering how little we had in common and how at the core, he was a pessimist and always felt hopeless. The realization that I was making a mistake didn't stop me. I consulted with my married friends, and they all talked about how much work marriage was and how it was often the women's role to be the backbone of a family and to nudge someone to change. That role had been ingrained in me from childhood. I spoke to my single friends but ignored their concerns. I woke up on the day we were to go to City Hall, aware of a gnawing intuition in my stomach which said, *don't do it.* I did it anyway.

Married and settled with a new place to call home, I returned to college part-time, got an entry level job in an office, and kept two bartending shifts. My new schedule was extremely taxing and my husband's constant cynicism weighed heavily on me. I woke up every day wishing I had listened to, as I like to call it, *my belly button.*

Six months after my wedding day, I was hospitalized and treated for MS only later to discover I had been misdiagnosed. My true diagnosis was a milder auto-immune disease, called neuro-retinitis. I had an inflamed optic nerve that resulted in blurry vision in my right eye. My husband was extremely concerned however, I felt very alone during my quest to recover and heal. I was interested in holistic remedies, wanting to make lifestyle changes to live a less financially stressful life. He was the opposite of that. He relied heavily on doing whatever we had to do to pay the bills and pressured me to take whatever the doctor prescribed. We were at odds with nearly everything.

I ignored my belly button again and did the exact opposite of taking care of myself. I poured myself into my studies and worked my way up the ladder at my desk job. One year later, I was promoted to administrative assistant, dropped out of college again, and was promoted for a second time, to executive assistant, shortly thereafter. The realization set in that I was capable of doing anything. I wanted to reach for the stars but my husband didn't want the stars. He was content with his life and very happy to have his television and whiskey every night. That was his happy place and although I was miserable, I kept it to myself. It dawned on me much later that I escaped living with an alcoholic father to being married to one.

Two years later, I finally opened up and told him how unhappy I was. He pleaded with me to stay and asked me what he could do to change my feelings. Reluctantly, he agreed to dream with me. We opened a restaurant together. Food is belonging, right? Or so I thought. I quit my job because after all, it wasn't my dream job. But neither was opening a restaurant. That was a dream I had *for him*.

I thought we would be a dream team. He would be in the kitchen cooking an incredible menu and I would run the business. Perhaps it would bring us closer together and maybe feed my soul in the process. I was trying to rescue him from a life he didn't want rescuing from. But I didn't know what I wanted for myself. I felt disconnected and broken. My mind and body were mismatched parts that struggled to operate in unison; I knew so little about myself. I never took the time to *know myself* as I had been always in survival mode for as long as I could remember. I pushed *him* because I was playing it small, hiding in his shadow, dreaming for him and not for myself.

In 2017, we opened the restaurant. Running it took its toll on me, physically especially because of my auto-immune disease. I was also mentally exhausted. The symptoms had gotten progressively worse due to my personal neglect and stress levels. Due to the pandemic, at the end of 2020 we closed the restaurant. It was a casualty of the many lockdowns. The decision to close the restaurant had nothing to do with the demise of our marriage, but it was very apparent during the three years of running it that our marriage wasn't working.

We had tumultuous fights. Marriage certainly didn't bring out the best in either one of us and, instead, magnified what wasn't working between us. Once the restaurant closed, we separated. We lost the business, filed for bankruptcy, and hit rock bottom. I was torn and ruminated back and forth on the idea of working things out to save the marriage. Eventually I came to the realization that I was grieving for the *comfort* of whatever *"home"* we would rebuild with each other. I intrinsically knew that if I stayed, we both would have been two broken souls merely struggling to survive. After a long deliberation, I left. It took a lot of courage and strength. The pandemic rescued me not only from my marriage but from myself.

BRAVE NEW WORLD

My dog, an eighty-five-pound Weimaraner, has played an instrumental part in my healing journey. Long walks with him have reconnected me to nature, which brought me joy and grounding from my childhood. We came into each other's lives at the perfect time. I had completely lost myself in the concrete jungle of NYC, so it was a gift to take mini trips to the ocean by car to watch the dog frolic on the beach so freely as the waves crashed; watching him filled my heart with peace and solitude. When we weren't at the beach, we would walk the trails in the woods. I've had so much time to notice there is no tree identical to another. I found freedom in the miniscule details of trees. These feelings have helped me heal physically, and also to surrender, release, live in complete gratitude, and rediscover my inner child.

There is a certain irony in the fact after everything I have done in my life to escape my parents' home, I moved back in with them at age thirty-nine. My father is ill and frail and I have assumed the caregiver role, for which I think my mother is grateful. In a sense, I have rescued her as they have me, by opening their home and allowing me to stay in what is such an uncertain time. There is so much for me to learn from being at rock bottom. I am genuinely happy not having anything, but I know it is time for me to finally discover myself, my voice, and this is part of my journey going forward.

As a child, I used to sit by the vast ocean and daydream. In my imagination, there lived a girl, the same age as me, trapped in the same place at the bottom of all those bodies of water: the ocean, the river, and the lake. Her hair was really long. It was so long that it floated to the surface from the depths of the waters, undulating with the waves. I felt she was sad, lonely, and had lost her voice. That's why she had fits; outbursts expressed as storms. This lost girl *was* the storm, she raged and rained on herself. As I reconnect with her now, something is different: I know how to save her.

The ocean is a central image.
It is the symbolism of a great journey.

ENYA

Trauma creates change you don't

choose. Healing is about creating

change you do choose.

MICHELLE ROSENTHAL

KRISTINA SHEA

Kristina Shea is a published author, founder of BlueSkys Life™ + Beauty, leading CBD expert, burnout coach, speaker and hope dealer. Her personal journey of loss, single parenthood, burnout and health challenges, prompted her path to healing emotionally and physically. During the pandemic, she pivoted from her thirty-year career in corporate America and founded her wellness company. Kristina pursued her mission to empower, build and educate women to prioritize their self-care, wellness and to "step into their skin" with confidence and vitality.

BLUE SKY LIFE

KRISTINA SHEA

*My experiences remind me that it's those black clouds
that make the blue skies even more beautiful.*

KELLY CLARKSON

I realized, soon after getting married, that as I made more money,
I had to work hard to help pay for our bills *and* for my husband's
toys. John always wanted the newest and best, whether video games
or *"big boy toys"* like motorcycles. He loved to ride but I always had
a dark feeling, a sixth sense that always told me this passion of his
would not have a good ending.

One day he brought home a shiny new, powerful, red Katana
motorcycle. I hated it. We had an explosive fight about his purchase
as he made it without telling me or without a discussion. But more
importantly, I felt John had brought the devil home.

On Saturday, April 5, 1997, John and I argued again about the
bike. I wanted him to sell it. I felt it was an expense and a danger.
I pleaded with no avail. He was determined to go riding the next

day as it was forecast to be an uncharacteristically warm, sunny day. I warned him to be careful of tired drivers as it would be the first day of daylight savings time. I suggested, *"Perhaps leave the bike at home? Wait for warmer weather?"* An angry heated discussion again ensued.

BLUE SKY STORM

That next morning was beautiful, it was a bright, sunny, blue-sky Sunday. I got up early to go to the office and hurriedly left our condo. John was playing video games with his back to me. Engrossed in his game, he didn't notice me, and I remember thinking I should say *"be careful"* and *"I love you."* I didn't say anything and dismissed the thoughts because in my mind I was late for the day ahead.

I wish so many times I could go back and at least say those five words. I used to think they may have changed the day, the outcome, or at least I would have said goodbye. Those unsaid words still haunt me.

Just a few hours later, John was hit head-on by a truck on a country road. His life ended and the life I knew was shattered. He was thrown from his bike to the side of a road, across from a farm. I do thank God there was a nurse that happened to be working at the mushroom farm that day. She cradled his head while he took his last breath; he was looking at that blue sky.

That afternoon, I had tried to call his cell to say *"I love you"* especially since we had argued the night before. I called several times. No answer. I was annoyed but kept working. Then I got a call from John's best friend's mother. *"Hello! How are you?"* I said, then paused awkwardly. *"Wait, how did you find this number?"* I asked and instantly knew something terrible had happened.

"There was an accident..." she began and I hung up on her and fell onto carpeted office floor. I called our condo and a police officer answered. I hung up. I didn't give him the chance to give me answer that I already knew. I then called his parents' house. Again, a police officer answered, so I hung up. Panic was building. I allowed his friend's mother to pick me up. While I waited, I pleaded with God to let John live. I went over bargains in my head—bartering with God to just let John be ok.

While she drove me to see John's parents, I was stricken with panic and fear like I have never known before—my heart pounded, my body shook, and my hands trembled. I opened the passenger door and ran across the green lawn where the snow had melted only the day before. A police officer stood there looking at me with a solemn expression—and I knew right then that what I feared was a reality.

I felt that blue sky spinning around me like a whirlwind. My legs no longer held me up. I collapsed and fell to my knees, screaming like a wounded animal on the front lawn of his parents' home. I could feel eyes on me, people coming out of their houses staring at this young blonde girl who had fallen into a heap of snow. I knew with no words being spoken I would never see my husband alive again. I was now a widow at twenty-four. I needed to identify my twenty-nine year old husband's body at the hospital. The bright blue sky turned into a dark looming storm.

When seeing John at the morgue, I screamed—the sounds seeming to vibrate throughout my entire body and reverberate around the entire space. To this day, I sometimes feel that sound is still stuck inside my body and chest, waiting to be fully released. I held his mangled and bloody body until I was torn from him by hospital staff. After seeing John playing video games in his underwear like a little kid only hours earlier, I identified his broken body in the morgue. Ribcage crushed, smashed teeth that once had a smile that used to make me melt. His face now had no life, no smile, no words to say—and the only thing that remained intact was the beautiful blue eyes that I had fallen in love with. I kept thinking this was his best joke ever. I expected him to get up and say I was such a dope for believing it. Going to bed that night, tripped up with pills the hospital gave me to calm me, I hoped that this was all a bad dream and I would wake up to a different reality.

BLUE EYES AND BLUE SKIES

The funeral and visitation were both long and drawn out. I stood exhausted and broken beside his casket, receiving condolences and people I didn't know advised me *"to be strong."* I wanted to scream at them to go away. I *was* being *strong*, I felt like yelling out to the world.

I barely remember the funeral except for fainting. So many people came out to send him off. I had John cremated as per his wishes (for some reason he had told me this) despite the Italian Catholic tradition. John's ashes are in a stain glass niche in a mausoleum overlooking a pond where the sunshine can stream in.

John's beautiful blue eyes were donated to a young boy who now has eyesight because of John's motorcycle accident. I like to think John can see the blue sky through this young man.

MIRROR, MIRROR ON THE WALL

I looked in the mirror. Who was this sad, shell of a person staring back at me? She was a stranger... did I ever know her? Without John, I seemed to be a shadow. I met him when I was fifteen. We grew up together, married and we were thinking of starting our own family.

My friends were John's friends. They simply disappeared after John passed so they were obviously *not* my friends. People avoided me as they didn't know what to say. I even had married girlfriends tell me they didn't like their husbands looking at me *that way* and to stay away. Then there were the men who thought I must be lonely and they propositioned me, wanting sex with me like vultures circling a kill. I felt totally alone and unwanted other than predatory men who saw in me a vulnerable target.

I tried to end my life with pills but at the last minute I decided to go the hospital to get my stomach pumped. I couldn't leave the world like that or do this to my parents even though they were not present in my life. Or could I? For some reason starving myself to death was easier. So, I consciously decided to stop eating. It reaffirmed I had no celebrations, no family, no *joy* left. I felt I didn't even *deserve* to eat, blaming myself for John's death. If I had just not gone to work that day, or stopped to say *"be careful"* instead of rushing out? Even John's mother lashed out at me, saying it was my fault he was dead. She even went so far to say John never loved me, attacking and judging every word and action of mine.

I didn't feel anyone would miss me anyway, maybe it was my fault. And not like I had friends, I told myself. I began to lose weight *fast* watching the scale to see how low I could go. I went from being around 125lbs to 81lbs.

My world was turned upside down, yet I was given only two weeks from work to grieve a lifetime for me with my husband. Our marital home was no longer mine as it had been sold. I couldn't even pack my condo. All our belongings were thrown into boxes randomly by some of John's friends. Our life together was reduced to disorganized beat-up cardboard boxes. I was in the depths of despair, feeling alone.

The rooms in the condo were spinning, I felt dizzy and unable to even talk. But I was screaming inside. I went to lie down outside and collapsed on the green grass. I rolled on my back and took note of birds chirping—looked up at the blue sky and the sun shining down. I felt some peace, and visualized John lying next to me, holding my hand. I cried and cried. People walked by staring at me, but no one came to offer a kind word. They just walked by, but for the first time I felt hope. That blue sky gave me hope. And to this day a blue sky speaks to me with peace, optimism, and strength. The blue sky became my talisman.

LOBSTER BISQUE LOVE

I knew Mike through work. He was dark and handsome, over ten years my senior, quiet and hardworking, He offered his sympathy and was a kind heart in a hard, uncaring office environment. He noticed that I had lost weight and my clothes were hanging on me. I looked like a walking skeleton. But by now, if I tried to eat, I was violently ill. Food previously meant family and love but was now the enemy of my body. I doubled over in pain if I ate anything solid.

Mike decided to help me eat. We took a road trip to Maine, and he started feeding me lobster bisque from a little diner by the ocean. He insisted I have spoonful each day and soon I was eating an entire bowl of decadent lovely bisque. Mike literally saved my life. I know in my heart I would have continued starving my body and my heart, if not for him.

I felt very nurtured and nourished. Every morning I went for walks along the beach, saw the sunrise and listened to the waves of the ocean. I started to feel myself healing. To this day, lobster bisque warms my heart.

I CAN FLY

My practical and logical thinking knew I had to deal with this depression and not through pills anymore. I learned that physical exercise was better than meds. Moving my body produced endorphins and serotonin, magical chemicals that could make me feel happy again.

I saw an ad in the newspaper which looked fun—belly dancing classes. I went to classes and watched performances and fell in love with the sensuous fluid movements, the glitter, swaying beads, and crystal costumes. I became obsessed. I was soon performing, teaching, and even toured Turkey with renowned dancers. I fell in love with the exotic and empowering dance and I could escape my pain while being someone else on stage. However, I was not escaping myself but truly finding myself. I was dancing into life.

I discovered these beautiful performance props, called Isis Wings. As soon as I saw these, I knew they were meant for me. They became part of my dance. I danced and floated powerfully with these wings. I felt lighter. I felt I could fly. I felt free.

KNOW WHEN TO WALK AWAY

Mike and I married. Yes, it was too soon. I craved love and he did too. I wanted the picture-perfect life that was taken from me but unfortunately, our marriage was not a good one. Mike had his own demons. I had stopped drinking to excess, but he had not. He was an alcoholic, chain smoker, and a gambler. Mike had social anxiety and was extremely depressed which led to violent outbursts and emotional abuse.

We did create a beautiful daughter together. He did his best as a father. I still loved him however his depression and emotional abuse became unbearable. It was destroying me and my soul. I had to leave one night during a very violent argument as I was in fear for my daughter and myself. To escape, I jumped on a plane to Montreal with my daughter. I told no one, not even my parents. I was embarrassed. I was so ashamed of the abuse I never told anyone what I was enduring. I was afraid my home would be burnt to the ground, but I still left.

I flew back many days later because I again received a phone call. It was Mike. *"Do you know what I did?"* he said. I was beside myself. I rushed to the hospital immediately after landing. The ER doctor told me Mike would not make it through the night. His words were surreal to me.

"What? Again? I'm losing Mike too? This is a bad dream. This cannot be real," I thought. Mike had tried to commit suicide. He made it through. However, he had serious damage to his body and the doctor told him he needed to stop drinking and smoking.

Mike was sick and needed help. I soon learned there was little support for mental health, so I took Mike back and nursed him to health despite all my friends saying I was crazy to take him home. I still loved him and needed to know he would be ok. But I had endured abuse for so long, I needed to save myself and my little girl. After he was stable, we separated but never divorced. He had left me with massive debt from gambling that I absorbed. I wanted him to be well and get back on his feet. It took some time, but we became close friends again over the years and I know he still loved me and I him.

FACEPLANT

I pushed myself to unimaginable limits, working ridiculous hours to keep my home, support my daughter, and pay off the huge debts. Typically, I slept three hours a night and used to say, *"I will sleep when I die."* Working full-time, I also had a freelance business, and taught dance in the evenings.

Going down the escalator on my way to meet a client, everything started spinning. I held the handrail. *Get a grip Kristina,* I thought to myself. Usually, the dizziness would pass. This time, as I took a step off the escalator, hit the floor, and everything went black. I heard people screaming for help and I was rushed to the hospital. I opened my eyes, but everything was black. I couldn't see. I panicked and thought *how can I work and provide for my daughter? Will I ever see her little cute face again?* Being in the dark was terrifying. Eventually I regained my eyesight. I had suffered migraines for years but convinced myself, *oh, it was just a bad migraine I'm fine.* I pushed the incident to the back of my mind.

After a multitude of tests, it was discovered that I had a brain cyst that put pressure on my brain causing migraines, and sleep issues. The neurosurgeon told me I needed to change my lifestyle and to consider surgery as an option. I chose not to operate because of risks associated with it.

The doctor told me if I don't sleep, I would die. I also needed to reduce my stress levels, as my blood pressure was very high and I was at high risk for a stroke. *"What?"* I said to him. *"I'm healthy!"* I always prided myself being fit, but I was pushing my body and mind to extremes he said. Working unrealistic hours for financial security was going to kill me. The neurosurgeon reminded me that if I was not here and alive, I would destroy any security for my daughter.

This was my wake-up call. I began an active pursuit of wellness which contributed to the shrinking of the brain cyst. I began to eat better, slept, and discovered meditation. I also started taking in the blue sky again. I had forgotten the power of those blue skies; I reconnected with a *"BlueSkys Mindset"*, as I call it.

TOUGH LOSSES

I received an early morning phone call. *"He's gone. Mike is gone."*

I fell to my knees. Mike died suddenly and was found on February 16th, 2016. I blamed myself, as I usually called him every Valentine's Day, and I didn't that year.

The absolute worst moment in my life was telling my daughter that her father passed away. I had to push my own grief and feelings aside. She was immediately physically ill. I held her close while she screamed like her heart had been ripped out. I totally understood her pain; the worst feeling as a mother is not being able to fix it. I couldn't put a band-aid and kiss it better. Her father was gone. The funeral was heart-wrenching. I had to watch my daughter suffer.

Within the same year, my own father passed away after a long and painful illness. I knew I was strong, but that strength was beginning to diminish. I seriously thought about ending my life. I cried and buried myself in bed for days, again putting my body through an extreme weight loss. I was so sick with stress and trauma, I couldn't even get up to get a drink of water. However, my purpose as a mother to my daughter got me through, and perhaps my own stubborn streak of not letting anything get the better of me. I was exhausted but I would never be broken.

TAKING FLIGHT

During the pandemic, from restructuring, I lost my job as a Senior Vice President of Marketing and Communications which was a catalyst to more life changes. Prior to losing my job, I had been overworking again and even ended up back in the ER. I was warned by the doctor: *"You have had two wake-up calls. You might not get another."*

I was totally *God-Smacked*. It was a sharp and hard slap across the face, as if God was saying, *Enough already! Just stop it, Kristina!*

I had lost both the financial security of my job and the certainty of my own physical health. I realized life that is too short to live on a hamster wheel going nowhere. I felt that I'm meant to be more than a corporate title, a job or even a mother. I had a heart and soul, and it was now beating and feeling again.

I had been giving to everyone else and I had been in fight or flight mode for over twenty years. My identity had become wrapped up in executive titles and the companies I worked for. I had become a workhorse, not dealing with my emotions, burying them deep within me. I had lost myself, but in doing so I found myself by healing my body. I was able to work on my inner self and I experienced a rebirth of my heart and soul. I realized that life is truly meant to be savored, (especially lobster bisque)!

I view my life experiences now as gifts. My pain became purpose, which made me resilient, strong, but also capable of love. When I look at the blue sky, I see hope and its unlimited vastness. It reaffirms to me that we have no limits. I'm now fueled with purposeful energy to live with intention, take flight into a new chapter of my life, and pickup my wings again to not only fly, but to soar.

If the sight of the blue skies fills you with joy,
rejoice, for your soul is alive.

ELEANORA DUSE

This life is mine alone. So I have stopped asking people for directions to places they've never been.

GLENNON DOYLE

CAITO STEWART

Caito Stewart is a published author, artist, sculptor, educator, and singer based in the New York area. After receiving her Bachelor of Fine Arts (BFA) in Painting in 2007, she moved to Tokyo where she taught English and then trained teachers at an English language school for nearly ten years. Caito earned a Master of Fine Arts degree (MFA) in Sculpture in 2020. Currently, she is the Director of Education at One River School of Art + Design. Caito enjoys spending her time hiking, working in her studio, and collaborating with her band, Das Yukon.

BUILDING WITH BROKEN BLUES

CAITO STEWART

*If you read the fine print, you will find that life
is subject to change without notice.*

NORA MCINERNY

THE ACCIDENT

"It's like we're in a movie!" I cried with excitement, as my older brother and I were outside on our friend's driveway watching Hurricane Floyd destroy houses and force drivers onto the roofs of cars. I was thirteen and naive, unaware this would lead to a more personal disaster a month later.

The phone rang as my older brother and I were making silly noises while doing homework in the family room. The gravity in Mom's voice interrupted our laughter. She shouted something about Andrew and rushed out the door. We anxiously awaited her return, unable to focus.

Andrew, our nine-year-old brother, was on a playdate when it happened. During the hurricane, a car had been swept into the ravine behind his friend's apartment complex, and the boys went looking for it. Andrew either lost his footing or the ground gave way, and he plummeted eighty feet. I assume the friend's parents called 911, because Mom never would have. She told us she arrived to see Andrew covered in blood and being loaded into a helicopter on a stretcher, still conscious and waving his arms. I can still conjure up a mental picture of that moment, as if I had seen it with my own eyes.

The last time I had been in a hospital, I had held a newly born Andrew as he sucked on my nose. This time, he was unconscious, and the doctors were trying to stop the bleeding and swelling in his brain. When they finally let us visit, I saw his blue eyes were open and grew hopeful. Even after I learned he was brain dead, and my parents decided to turn off life support, I expected him to wake up. I was optimistic, as he was breathing on his own before we went home that night.

CHRISTIAN SCIENCE

Before Andrew died, I already felt different from my peers at public school, although I'm sure we seemed like any other middle-class family living in the suburbs of New York. What they didn't know was that we were Christian Scientists.

I owe my existence to Christian Science, or CS for short. My parents were both born and raised in it and met at college. The religion was founded in Boston in the late 1800s by Mary Baker Eddy, when medicine was still primitive. The popularity of CS grew out of the belief that anyone could heal themselves through prayer, just like Jesus. Of course, medicine had advanced spectacularly, and even to me it seemed pretty weird that we refused medical care.

Despite my embarrassment at school, CS was my religion and way of life; I was raised to view it as truth. I had been taught we had an advantage: medicine would not be as effective or permanent a solution as CS prayer. My mom tried to keep us ignorant of the physical world, muting medicine commercials and avoiding TV shows featuring illness or hospitals. Instead of *"I have a cold,"* I had been taught to say, *"I have the belief of a cold."* The logic was that learning about illness or acknowledging its existence would make it seem real, and harder to vanquish.

Regardless of his supposed devotion to CS, I noticed my dad talked about diseases a lot. Whenever I felt sick, he would tell me to wash my hands and stay away. To maintain his impeccable physique, he lifted weights and followed a strict exercise and diet regime. This was the best way to avoid heart disease, diabetes, or cancer, he would say, before commenting, *you could lose some weight.*

Dismissive of dieting or exercise, my mom stocked the kitchen with foods forbidden at friends' houses. We would snuggle up on the couch, watching movies with giant bowls of ice cream and popcorn. Looking back, I realize food was the only physical comfort she allowed herself, and it taught me to eat as a coping mechanism.

Being sandwiched between these opposing values was confusing and stressful. No matter what I chose to do, I disappointed one parent or the other. If I ignored my mom's obesity, it was easier to side with her than my dad, since the pressure to conform to his high physical standards was difficult. I decided she was morally superior, and right about everything.

GUILT, SHAME AND ABANDONMENT

CS made Andrew's death even more shocking and confusing. When I was scared in the hospital that day, my parents reminded me that if we remembered Andrew was a perfect, spiritual idea of God, he would be healed. The physical body was unreal, life was eternal, and death was impossible. I was surprised that my parents had a memorial service for Andrew, but the rest of their approach was typical of Christian Scientists: never seeing the body, swift cremation and scattering of the ashes, and avoiding talk of death or grief. Funerals, graves, cemeteries, and urns were part of another world that believed in death. My dad promptly donated Andrew's belongings, turning his toy-filled bedroom into a bland, characterless guest room. The door was kept closed. Apart from a framed photo on the dresser of him kayaking, there was no evidence of his existence. We almost never mentioned him again, even on his birthday or death anniversary.

All this silence led to ignorance, confusion, guilt, and shame. My mother, brother and I all felt responsible, believing we had somehow undermined the efficacy of Andrew's CS treatment. I hadn't believed enough, my mom had let him be taken to a hospital, and Rob, my older brother, was convinced his doubts about CS were the problem.

Unbeknownst to me, at the time, the guilt consumed Rob until he decided to stop believing in CS. When he told my mom why he would no longer be attending church, her reply was,

"Well, if that's the case, then we can't love each other anymore, because Christian Science is who I am." Instead of supporting him and validating his pain, she rejected and emotionally abandoned him.

From my perspective, it seemed like someone had flipped a switch and suddenly my brother was always angry. No one thought I needed to know why. When my parents said they didn't know, I believed them. I noticed he stopped coming to church and my mom didn't nag him about it, but I never understood why she always seemed to bear the brunt of his rage. Terrified he might redirect his anger at me, I hid in my bedroom. Once something set him off, the day was ruined and everything put on hold, while my parents tried and failed to placate him. Even on *"normal"* days, he seemed to get all the attention, and I had to go entire meals or car rides without getting to speak. I swallowed my resentment and convinced myself I wasn't worthy of being listened to anyway.

CONDITIONAL LOVE

From a young age, I had learned that love was conditional. They would often say how grateful they were that I was a happy, sweet, good kid. When I admitted to feeling depressed or anxious, they would tell me that I was a perfect child of God and nothing could be wrong. They advised me to list things I was grateful for so I would realize how perfect life was. I interpreted all this to mean that I had to always be perfect; making mistakes or feeling negative emotions would make me undeserving of love or respect. The few times I got in trouble in elementary school,

I was desperate to reclaim my *"good girl"* status, and tearfully confessed in the hopes that my mom would still love me.

In high school, my submissive, people-pleasing behavior spilled into my social life. The thought of breaking with CS and lying to my mom meant I would at first say no when invited out for drinks or to parties, yet I caved into peer pressure and did it anyway. Fearing rejection, I avoided conflict, molded myself to be who I thought others wanted me to be, and never expressed opinions, needs, or desires. Boyfriends dumped me and friends complained about my passivity and indecisiveness, and I felt helplessly doomed to be an apologetic doormat. All I wanted was to be loved and accepted.

LESSONS IN PEOPLE PLEASING

My favorite place was the art room in high school, but my artistic prowess couldn't cure my low self-esteem. I internalized the idea that what I loved and excelled at was less valuable or important, especially when my dad kept suggesting that I should study something more lucrative, and classmates commented, *"I guess you'll have to marry a rich doctor."* If my mom and art teacher hadn't encouraged me to go to art school, I doubt I would be an artist today.

I chose to study art at Washington University in St. Louis for three reasons: the campus was pretty, it was far from my family drama, and I hoped to find like-minded people. I joined the Christian Science Organization (CSO), but there were only three other members. After an art school friend saw me handing out CS flyers on campus and called me *"creepy,"* I dragged my feet to the weekly meetings, although I was too afraid to quit for fear of Mom's disapproval.

Equally eager to please in my art classes, I compared myself to classmates and changed my work to fit others' ideals. After a professor nominated me to apply for a prestigious summer program in my junior year, my elation turned to shame when my application was rejected. I stopped painting and pushed my professors and classmates away. After a year of confusion and despair, I finally found a suitable motif for contrasting the beautiful and grotesque in life: meat. I unleashed my repressed sexuality, anger, and grief through quick, juicy strokes of messy, globby oil paint.

The meat paintings proved polarizing, and it was the first time I realized I couldn't please everyone—that I needed to create for myself. Unfortunately, whenever I tried to paint after college, I couldn't get the other voices out of my head. I felt art school had robbed me of the joy, solace, and identity I had once found in art.

FINDING MYSELF IN JAPAN

I considered teaching art after college but was unsure if I would like it. My mom suggested I try teaching English in Japan. I fully expected to come back after one year, but life had other plans. Ever since a girl called me a freak in fifth grade, I had tried to hide my inner goofy kid who performed for friends during recess. I knew I could let her out again after I instinctively pretended to gobble up plastic fruit as if I was Cookie Monster, and my four-year-old students laughed so hard that snot flew out of their noses. By the end of every class, I was usually soaked in sweat, and the children were smiling and high-fiving me. I felt like a rock star.

When a trainer position at headquarters opened up five years later, I was confident enough to apply and get the job. I was responsible for training new teachers, watching their lessons, and helping them improve their teaching. As soon as I started, I was terrified people would find out I wasn't a perfect teacher, and confiding in a co-worker only left me more embarrassed and alone. Bent on improving, I researched techniques, tried them out on my students, and practiced training presentations at home. My confidence and passion for the work grew, and I shifted my focus to helping others. This helped me clarify my values, learn to be more assertive, and take more initiative. I garnered trust and respect, as I worked to push through discomfort, model vulnerability and empathy, and support others through challenges.

EMBRACING MEDICINE

Unfortunately, my new role required desk work, and I developed a herniated disc. Bed-ridden with excruciating pain, I called my mom, who suggested I call a CS practitioner. I paid them to pray for me, while I hunkered down and read the passages they recommended from the CS textbook, *Science and Health*. The language was old-fashioned and hard to understand.

When I sheepishly reported no change in my condition, the practitioner seemed frustrated and asked me what erroneous thoughts I was having, if I was drinking alcohol, or if I was having pre-marital sex. At almost thirty years old, I didn't think these things were her business, but she had hit a nerve and confirmed my worst fear: It was my fault. I was bad, unworthy of healing, health, or love.

Humiliated and desperate for relief, I gave up on CS and saw a doctor. Though the experience was unfamiliar and scary, I was amazed how well the medications worked. Once my pain lessened, my dad gave me a workout routine to strengthen my core and protect my spine. For the first time, I felt grateful for his extensive knowledge about health and fitness. The guilt, however, for failing to heal myself, breaking with CS, and disappointing my mother, would continue to gnaw at me.

CHANGING PRIORITIES

Don't be afraid of your fears. They're not there to scare you. They're there to let you know that something is worth it.

C. JOYBELL C.

I had started painting after a couple years in Japan, but once I received a promotion and a new boyfriend, it fell by the wayside. Three years later, I was in crisis again after a cancer scare that turned out to be the mumps, and then getting dumped a month later. Completely shattered, I started painting a still-life arrangement of blue and white pottery shards I had collected from Japanese beaches, which I called "Broken Blues." Observing and replicating their beautiful imperfections helped me heal; it felt like a metaphor for putting myself back together. That year, painting helped me cope with a slew of personal and professional disappointments, as I helped my team weather a major restructuring. Though I grew as a leader, I sensed I was approaching a ceiling of professional opportunity.

During our regular Skype call, I confided in my mom that I wanted to make art a higher priority again. She suggested returning for grad school, but I doubted I would fit back into American society. Plus I was afraid I didn't have what it took to be a professional artist. I was also nearing the ten year-mark in Tokyo, when I would become eligible for Permanent Residency, and I had done so many things in Japan I never thought I could do. In addition to my professional achievements, I had overcome stage fright, writing and performing songs as the lead singer in a rock band. I had studied Japanese and passed the highest level of the Japanese Language Proficiency Test. I had tons of close friends, and loved visiting the art museums, restaurants, bars, coffee shops, karaoke joints, hot springs, and hiking spots around Tokyo. I was also attached to my studio apartment, decorated with care. Japan was my home now. Leaving, I thought, was impossible.

THE TURNING POINT

When my mom unexpectedly died, everything seemed to fall apart. I was on the first day of a ten-day solo trip to tropical Okinawa, and left immediately for New York. After a couple weeks, I was eager to return home to Tokyo, but my left leg was swollen and numb when I got off the plane. Doctors couldn't find a cause, but I couldn't walk or go to work, and I began having panic attacks. To my surprise, my brother and his wife dropped everything to come take care of me.

When they left a week later, my leg still wasn't healed, and I felt that my priorities had shifted. I was awakened to the realization that life was short and all interest in my job in Japan had melted away.

If I wanted to be an artist, I needed to be one now. No matter how scary, I knew I needed to face my past and prove to myself that I could be this new person in my home country. After I told a friend my thoughts, my leg started working again. Encouraged by this somatic affirmation, I set up a meeting with HR, and broke the news with tears streaming down my cheeks.

BACK IN NEW YORK

Ten years after graduating university, I was starting over again. I was living at my parents' house and trying to figure out my next steps. Like the nose piercing I had neglected while in Japan, the hole of my absence that I had left in New York had closed up years ago. Re-piercing old scar tissue was painful, but doing so through layers of grief, reverse culture shock, and a pile of secondary losses was doubly so. I had lost my apartment, job, income, friends, and identity.

My old friends in New York had lives I didn't fit into anymore, and it was hard knowing I had a perfect life back in Japan. If I returned, I wouldn't have to re-learn how to drive a car, follow Western table manners, engage in small talk, tip service workers, or guard against pickpockets. I wouldn't have to unlearn bowing, slurping noodles, picking up bowls to get the last grain of rice, and leaving my bags unattended. The only problem: Japanese Immigration had punched a hole in my card, meaning I had relinquished my right to reside there.

I tried to carve out a new space for myself in New York. I painted, applied to graduate school, joined bereavement groups, salvaged old, neglected friendships, moved to Brooklyn, and got a new boyfriend. Eventually, I stopped finding the faults in New York and started finding things to appreciate, and slowly, I began to let go of Japan.

I AM AN ARTIST

In my first month back, I attended a retreat on shadow work, where I discovered I was unable to say, *"I am an important artist,"* without crying. Entering the MFA program at Pratt Institute a year later helped me claim this part of myself, and my artwork changed drastically.

For years, I had obscured my grief with abstraction, but now it was raw and unavoidable, and people couldn't seem to connect with that approach. When I tried a more direct approach, I was told not to get so personal. Professors battered me in critiques, leaving me frozen, tongue-tied, and curled in a ball. I felt increasingly frustrated, misunderstood, and alone, and knew I was slipping into the same patterns from undergrad, but I didn't know how to stop it.

Exacerbating the situation was the news that my dad was remarrying and selling our childhood home. The panic attacks continued, and by the end of first semester, I was considering quitting. My grief counselor suggested medication to help manage my depression and anxiety, so I could get through school. My ability to feel joy was restored, and my anxiety and depression became manageable.

Thankfully, I continued with school, and soon discovered I was a sculptor. I enjoyed how the intense, tactile labor of sculpting conceptually reflected the work of grief. Though people's discomfort with grief triggered my insecurity, I resisted the urge to stop making and talking about my work. I had seen first-hand in my support groups that community and connection were validating and healing, and this emboldened me to tell my story more openly. I wanted to normalize discussion of trauma, grief, and loss.

I was also deconstructing my CS upbringing, and the act of talking and making art about both grief and my religious recovery felt rebellious. I was angry that my mom had kept her heart attacks, strokes, and pancreatitis a secret from me, worrying that my fear would undermine her CS treatment. I resented that CS had influenced us to eschew mourning customs meant to bring the comfort and closure I still craved over twenty years after Andrew's death. With the help of my support groups, I learned my self-worth wasn't tied to others' approval, and that I could set boundaries, my neurons could be rewired, and I could unlearn shame, perfectionism, and people-pleasing. I didn't have to be that person anymore.

When COVID hit during my last semester, classes went online, my thesis show was canceled, and I lost access to my studio. Still, I was determined to finish my sculptures, especially Ghost Tike Part 1: A Memorial for Andrew. While cleaning out my childhood home, I had learned my parents had scattered his ashes under our favorite climbing tree, the Japanese maple in the front yard. Now it felt like we had left him behind. As an alternate DIY memorial, I had started making Japanese maple leaves out of paper and paint. Longing for connection during the lockdowns, I offered virtual leaf-crafting workshops, where I shared my story and invited people to join in my grief ritual. A month later, I participated in the Art in Odd Places 2021: NORMAL, a performance festival in Manhattan, where I invited people to join me in person.

When Ghost Tike and my other sculptures were finally exhibited in April 2021, I had already made over 5,500 leaves, which overflowed from a used toddler car. I was happy to share Andrew's story and help others in grief, but truly relished the closure I felt when Rob and I held hands posing for a photo with our brother's memorial sculpture.

I CAN DO HARD THINGS

When a broken vessel is reconstructed in the Japanese art of Kintsugi, the cracks are sealed with lacquer and dusted with gold, a lesson in embracing our imperfections. All of my artwork, including "Broken Blues," similarly reminds me that each time my own life has fallen apart, I have used my art practice to gather up the shards and rebuild. There's no guarantee I won't break again, but now I know I can put myself back together. Awareness of my own resilience helps me persist in being vulnerable and taking risks. I still struggle with fear, insecurity, and shame, but the less I hide my scars, the more I empathize and connect with others. With each transformation, I get a little bit closer to being more fully myself: an important artist, inherently worthy of love.

Vulnerability is the birthplace of innovation, creativity and change.

BRENÉ BROWN

"

It is so important to take time for yourself and find clarity. The most important relationship is the one you have with yourself.

DIANE VON FÜRSTENBERG

MARIYA TARASIO

Mariya Tarasio is a published author, a 2017 Recipient of the Brilliant Minded Woman Award, philanthropist and professionally has been an Executive Assistant for over twenty years. She has always had a "whatever it takes" attitude. Her volunteer work with non-profits and her EA roles have led her to coordinate large scale events including fashion shows and conferences. Mariya has a passion for helping others and has assisted many families globally to start their lives and careers in Canada which has given her great joy. When she is not with her young adult children, her weekends are spent supporting seniors ensuring they are active and engaged.

SPINE OF STEEL

MARIYA TARASIO

A life spent making mistakes is not only more honorable,
but more useful than a life spent doing nothing.

GEORGE BERNHARD SHAW

I was raised in a traditional Italian home where family was a principal value. We all gathered weekly and that was the commitment that kept us close knit. The best place to do this was around a massive table that included not only my parents, my brothers, and me; however, on occasion, neighborhood kids and other extended family also circled that table. Our house was always bustling with friends and relatives popping by. Being the only girl, there was absolutely no way I could get out of helping prepare our weekly expression of love and community: the food.

Life for me was pretty simple. I was considered a quiet, *"good girl."* I was the one that listened to her parents, never challenged anything they said, suggested, or demanded. Everything in my life had been planned out from childhood: I would finish high school, work, get married, and have children. Getting married and having children were the ultimate goals. Once I became a wife and mother, my life would be complete, and I couldn't wait for the day that it was my table that I was placing homemade meals on, for my husband, children, friends, and family. All I wanted was to create a food marathon for the ones that I loved the most, and I was going to get there. There was no thought of post-secondary school studies. A mom was more than enough for me to be and being the best at it was my definition of success.

CROSSROADS IN SILENCE

The turning point in the process of growing up is when you discover the core of strength within you that survives all hurt.

MAX LERNER

One of my happiest days, one I spent my lifetime preparing for, was my wedding day. In my head, it was all so romantic: the idea of two families coming together to celebrate a lifelong, sacred union. I was ready for a marriage where the man is the voice, the decision maker, the protector, and the leader. Yes, I know that it was old-fashioned, but I was ok with it. I mean... *there isn't anything more to life...* or so I thought at the time.

The sense of accomplishment was one of the best feelings for me at the time. My self-esteem soared, before then, I wasn't even aware that my self-worth and self-esteem needed validating. It was not so much a feeling at all, as it was the absence of the fear of failure. So, I continued to do what I believed was expected of as a wife. And things felt good.

So, when did it all go wrong? It is difficult to pinpoint the exact timeframe. Were there red flags at the beginning of the marriage? Yes, but I ignored them. Was it after I had my two children within two years of each other? All I can say is that something inside me shifted. I began to feel differently about my life. I realized that being that wife and mother, which was supposed to be my end goal and the path to ultimate happiness, was not enough for me. I loved being a mother. But in the marriage? Well, it felt like there was a lot missing. To me, it felt like I had been ripped from the core of what I liked about myself, like some outside force drained me of all my energy. I realized that I had lost myself. I missed the simple little girl I once was. I knew that I signed up for this life, and my life was what was exactly as had thought I wanted. However, I had not known beforehand of the toll being in the backseat of my own life would take on me. I had no voice. I felt that I didn't matter and nothing that I contributed to the marriage and my little family mattered. My self-worth and self-esteem plummeted.

I believe when two people's energies align, they gravitate to each other. We call this chemistry. However, if energies clash, as they did between my husband and I, then they just push each other away. There are so many moving parts within a relationship: there is a part that wants motivation to work on the other goals and why shouldn't there be a part that wants excitement? Are there parts that want to be left alone? There are certainly parts that are broken and sometimes I was unable to identify where the broken parts came from.

My brain swirled with uncertainty and many questions. *Do I leave? How do I leave? What do I do when I leave and where do I go? How do I manage with nothing?* I had my two little children to think about, not just myself but I knew that I had to go. This crossroad pushed me to a place I never thought I would ever been in. All my beliefs and childhood dreams of what I thought I wanted were challenged. I was in fear for both my future and my children's if I left. *What would my family say?*

Yet, I did the unthinkable and left. To save myself, I went against the narrative I was raised with. I went into the great unknown with my two small children. Deep down I knew it was the right thing, but I was terrified. I didn't let my fear stop me as I realized that I couldn't live the life I was living.

IN COLD BLOOD

The Universe has your back even when things aren't working out the way you expected.

GABRIELLE BERNSTEIN

Am I awake? Is this my nightmare? I opened one eye and squinted, ever so slightly, through the other. Lying on a mountain of snow on that unforgettable night in January, I felt blood running down my neck. Is the blood mine? *Is the blood cold or am I cold from laying in this snow?* I was in shock.

"GET UP!" The words blasted in my ear. His voice reverberated like a million octave ranges of rage. He dragged me by my hair to the car and shoved me into the passenger seat to make our

way back to his house. I prayed he would not notice as I slipped my hand into my purse searching for my keys. I had to get out of the car. I stopped myself from grabbing the door handle and jumping out of the moving vehicle. *"I am a single mom, I am a single mom, I am a single mom,"* were words that I chanted silently in my head so he wouldn't see my fear. This altercation was the result of me talking to someone at his birthday party, a celebration with friends. How could I have allowed someone to dictate whom I was apparently *"allowed"* to speak with?

This wasn't the first time that I had allowed Nick to put me in a place of uncontrollable fear. It had been months of escalated rage from him. With my keys in my hand, I struck Nick hard enough across his chest to leave a considerable mark. *"Let me out of this car!"* I shouted as loud as I could.

With insane rage Nick screamed, *"We are going to the police! You just scratched me with your keys,"* and within what seemed like a split second, he viciously turned the car around and sped his way to police station. Once we were in the parking lot, the car idled, and I reached for the car door handle to open it. Unfortunately, I wasn't fast enough. I felt the blunt force of his arm across my chest, as he sought to prevent me from exiting the car. Nick peeled out of station parking lot and headed towards his house.

We arrived at his house and I was determined to grab my overnight bag and go home. In hindsight, I should have just left the bag, and got into my car that was parked on the driveway; I should have left then, but I didn't. That proved to be a big mistake. Nick's rage was beyond terrifying, he was now at the point of hysteria. I had never experienced this in my life. He grabbed me from behind and placed a knife to my throat and gun to my head. My thoughts raced, *"How do I get out of here?"* I thought. *"My kids need me—God, please get me out of here!"*

Nick kicked me repeatedly in my back, and then tossed me down the stairs. Somehow, I mustered up enough strength to free myself from his grip. I ran out of the house straight into my car. By this time, tears and dried blood covered my face, snow still falling, and I sped through slippery, icy roads. How I reached home seems like divine inspiration. It was 5:00 am January 5th.

At home, I didn't even try and sleep. I couldn't. At 9:00 am someone who had been at the party called me.

"Mariya, are you ok?"

I couldn't reply. The words were stuck in my throat.

"Mariya, I saw what happened, you need to go to the police."

Hesitantly, I said, *"Just let me figure it out, I'm scared. Please don't push me to do anything right now because I am scared."*

EMOTIONS IN CHECK

"This is Constable Hogan. Is this Mariya Tarasio?"

"Yes, it is." I replied.

"I need you to come to the station," the officer said.

It was around 12:15 pm on Saturday afternoon. Frozen in fear, in pain from my injuries, I changed clothes and made my way to meet Constable Hogan. Upon my arrival, I was guided into a small room. The pungent smell of bleach filled the air. To this day, that smell triggers memories of that awful night. A police officer photographed and a doctor examined and measured my bruises and scratches. The measuring tape felt like it was made of ice. On video, for my official police statement, I had to relive every detail of the last twelve horrendous hours.

"Thank you Mariya," said Constable Hogan afterwards.

"Now what do I do?" I asked.

"Nothing. We are going to arrest him and all you have to do is wait for us to contact you with the day that you need to show up in court."

Another rush of fear flooded through me as I anticipated having to face Nick in front of a judge, the police who took my video recorded statement, the doctors that assessed me when I went to the station, but worst of all, I feared all this happening in front of my mother—the woman who knows me as a good, quiet, calm little girl that never caused heartache or pain. I dreaded the call and the letter announcing the court date.

The court date was secured months later and I knew that I couldn't go alone. I needed my mother. She was the closest person to me and my biggest support.

PANIC TO POWER

Entering the courtroom, a wave of panic set in as I was forced to see and hear the man that felt it was ok to do this to me. I had to relive all of it with this insane fear all over again. *Sentenced to prison* were the lyrics to the song I wanted so badly to hear. And I heard them. But then I wondered, *"What is he going to do to me when he gets out of prison?"* Yes, he was put behind bars so he couldn't hurt me, or anyone else for that matter.

As time went on, I started to feel lighter, the world became brighter. My panic turned to empowerment, I started to really think about how one starts to believe in themselves again after trauma. How does one put the many experiences of being in this kind of toxic unhealthy and poisonous relationship behind them?

I began to set aside everything that didn't matter and that didn't serve a positive purpose. I started to put myself in situations where I could learn and grow. However, my past put a stop to my growth, as I was often triggered and would be reminded, again and again, of the series of events that took place. For six months into my journey, I was not able to walk, crawl, or even move without excruciating pain. I didn't know where the pain came from.

"Mariya, you need back surgery, we can't fix this without surgery. Were you in a car accident recently?" asked the medical professional I consulted about the pain. *"Are you in a physically abusive relationship that you would like to share with us? The damage done to your spine must be the result of one of either of these two."* So, of course, I had to share with the surgeon my past experiences of physical abuse.

On January 17, 2017, at 7:00 am I was scheduled for back surgery. Five discs needed to be replaced because of the damage. I knew that I was going to be ok. At least that was what I kept telling myself. I would have a new back and with this new back, I would be able to walk taller in confidence, emotion, and strength.

The surgery was successful and the next steps were that I had to learn how to walk all over again. In my mind, I was determined. *I can and I will and I did* was my affirmation statement.

With cane in hand and coordinating event after event as part of my new business to help other women, I was not going to let the cane get in the way of my event commitments. I was not going to let the cane get in the way of ensuring my children were taken care of. I was not going to let the cane stop me from driving, stop me from pushing, or stop me from doing whatever I needed to do in order to move forward with grace, determination, and integrity.

HOPE AND FAITH

Without experiences and struggles in our journey, we may not grow. It is these obstacles and lessons that help us become who we are meant to be. Did I give up when life got difficult? No; it strengthened me. I was able to not only overcome but to rise. My choices and circumstances gave me the backbone to find my voice and power. I realize that nothing can hold me back.

There is not one of us who is immune to challenges. How we handle those challenges determines what defines us. It's never too late to become who you want to be and who you can become authentically. Through the years, I have discovered so much and I continue to uncover more of who I am. Although circumstances in my life and choices I made didn't have the outcome I desired, still the Universe lead me the right path. Even in my greatest fear and despair, I never lost hope or faith that things would work out as they should. I incorporated my lessons and became stronger as a result. The lesson is that we shouldn't let a moment in time, a circumstance that you may find yourself in, or another's opinion become that definition. Instead, keep the faith and know in your heart that it is you who ultimately determines your worth.

She will rise; with a spine of steel
and roar like thunder, she will rise.

NICOLE LYONS

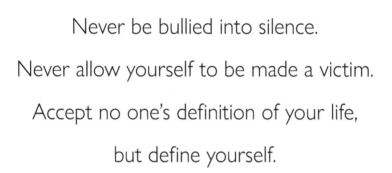

Never be bullied into silence.

Never allow yourself to be made a victim.

Accept no one's definition of your life,

but define yourself.

HARVEY FIERSTEIN

ACKNOWLEDGMENTS

NATASHA AZADI

Special gratitude goes to my friend, Soul Coach and Medium, Debra. Without your support and guidance I would never have had the courage to find my voice to tell my story. Because of you, I can go forward and help so many others.

All my love,

Natasha

DR. CRAIG BEACH

This chapter is dedicated to my mother, Donna, whose role modeling, unwavering support, and unconditional love provided the critical foundation upon which I have been able to become the man I am today.

A special shout out to Dr. Cary Cuncic, Kate Jordan, and Stephanie Robinson; you know the real me and have embraced and accepted me through it all which, in turn, has allowed me to continue to soar beyond my wildest dreams. THANK YOU!

LISA CARTER

Mom, thank you for always believing in me and never putting any limits on what you thought I could accomplish.

To my wonderful children, Robert, Kristina and Alycia. Each of you are so different, yet all three of you complete my heart. You are the fuel that keeps me moving forward. I am so proud of each of you.

Ava and Claire, you taught me a whole new level of unconditional love. You are my world. I am so blessed to be your Mimi.

Ben, thank you for the being the 'crazy' glue that keeps us all together.

Lastly, to Carol Starr Taylor from Star House Publishing Inc., for your guidance and support throughout this journey.

KIM MURPHY

I have been blessed with three strong and amazing daughters: Sydney, Devon and Morgan who I love dearly and thank daily for their love, life-lessons and spirits. I could not have done any of it, without you.

KRISTINA SHEA

I would like to dedicate this chapter in loving memory to my husbands, John and Mike.

To my daughter Chloé, thank you for always being my shining light. I am so proud of the young woman you have become.

Thank you to Carol Starr Taylor of Star House Publishing Inc. for helping me share my story.

Finally, I would like to thank all of you for reading my story and I hope it has inspired you to live your BlueSkys Life™!

CAITO STEWART

I dedicate this chapter to both my mother, Marti, and little brother, Andrew.

To my dad John, brother Rob, and sister-in-law Meli, thank you, for your love and support.

Thank you to my best friend and partner, Oliver.

To my forever friends, thank you for your camaraderie, love, and support: Renee, Myra, Anne, Eva, Ale, Jesse, Rachel, Amy, Christine, Becca, Fran, Takako, Lene, Akari, Joy, the Motherless Daughters, Dinner Partiers, Ex-Christian Scientists, Usha, Lynn, Alex, Norma, Leslie C, and so many others.

MARTIN REID

I would like to dedicate my chapter to my late parents, Matt and Maureen Reid.

To Julie, thank you for always being there for me. You have been a major influence in my life.

To my three kids Calvin, Jacqueline and Graham, I am so proud of each of you. I am grateful and blessed that we have been able to build something wonderful together.

A special thank you to all of you that have helped me become who I am today.

CARL RICHARDS

Thank you to my fifth grade teacher Mrs. Pipe for suggesting Speech Therapy. Who knows how different my life would have been if I hadn't been introduced to it.

To my parents, John and Jeannine for their continued love and support.

Thank you to my husband Jeff for always believing in me and walking life's journey together.

My sincerest gratitude to all my other family and friends who continue to support me along the way.

LISA RIZZO

I want to give special thanks to all of you that have supported me over the years. My journey has not gone without its hard times, here and beyond. But when you share your positive energy with others that are willing to share back, we grow stronger in our journey together. For that, I am grateful.

STEPHANIE ROBINSON

This chapter is dedicated to the memory of my step-mother Monica.

Thank you to my family, mentors, and friends who "just get me." I have been so lucky to have your love, support, guidance, comfort and encouragement through all the laughter and the tears. You believed in me when I didn't believe in myself. This story could have ended very differently if it were not for the fact you ALL loved the HELL out of me... literally and figuratively!

ROE SARITA

My deepest gratitude to Carol Starr Taylor at Star House Publishing Inc., for the coaching and guidance. Her expertise in NLP proved to be instrumental in my writing process because I didn't know the story of my life. I thought I knew, but I didn't. Carol's techniques expanded my perception of my reality and allowed me to develop an understanding of myself and my place within this world. Thank you Carol Starr Taylor!

MARIYA TARASIO

Thank you to my parents, Guiseppina and Salvatore, for a childhood filled with remarkable memories and for giving me the truest value of family.

To my brothers, Oliver and Danny and sister-in-law, Victoria, who always kept me pushing.

I am eternally grateful for the gift of my children. Gabriel and Noah, you both keep me encouraged, hungry to grow and keep going. I am inspired by your passion and drive every day.

Thank you Alex for believing in me, and showing me there is no remedy for love, the gift is loving more.

9 781989 535547